IT'S **ONLY** MONEY—
MEMORY IS THE TRUE VALUE

IT'S **ONLY** MONEY—
MEMORY IS THE TRUE VALUE

Musings of a Journey Past

HAROLD A. FONROSE, M.D., F.A.C.P.

iUniverse, Inc.
Bloomington

IT'S **ONLY** MONEY—**MEMORY** IS THE TRUE VALUE
Musings of a Journey Past

iUniverse books may be ordered through booksellers or by contacting:

iUniverse
1663 Liberty Drive
Bloomington, IN 47403
www.iuniverse.com
1-800-Authors (1-800-288-4677)

ISBN: 978-1-4697-0934-5 (sc)
ISBN: 978-1-4697-0936-9 (hc)
ISBN: 978-1-4697-0935-2 (ebk)

Printed in the United States of America

iUniverse rev. date: 02/05/2012

Cover photo of Four Roads Trolley by Stephen Dalla Costa.

CONTENTS

DEDICATION

T HIS DEDICATION IS INTENDED FOR women in general but two specifically:

My grandmother in this sense is a main personage. Her personality infuses the beginning of my formative years in such force that she stands as the point of departure to the recent past and on to the present.

Of similar but different importance is my wife, Betty. Betty joined the journey in 1956. From that moment my life's narrative assumed a different form. My studies and performance in medical school became more structured and probably increased in performance. Certainly the financial aid provided greater stability. As the time passed, her role in forming the present family cannot be overestimated.

Indeed, Betty's role could not be overstated. There is her constant presence since joining the journey in medical school and the multi-tasking role of initiating a family-focus with four sons and the burgeoning activity of a wide-ranging professional career to its completion of my medical leadership as a medical director.

My favorite memory is an early snapshot of her at the beginning of the family circle where she is reading to two of the younger children. Her concentration and focus symbolizes her structural role in a six-member family. Indeed, there is no overstatement of the positive impact throughout the journey since joined in 1956.

Further, Betty's contribution to the book over the past four to five months has been outstanding. Several of the sections were read to her for testing the validity and the completeness of any ideas expressed.

Frequently, she would add instances to improve both the structure and content of the narrative.

Indeed *the* journey became *our* journey to what is now a 55-year partnership. The co-dedication is both natural and complete in terms of Betty and her contribution to this book.

FOREWORD

T HE FACT THAT DR. FONROSE ("Harold") would commit to chronicle his life to "ink" is remarkable! For to know him, and I've had the privilege of knowing him now for decades, is to know a man who is fiercely private and focused on his life's work. He is not one who lives in the past or who seeks validation of himself. His writing reflects an objective, almost clinical, reporting of his life's journey.

In this regard, Dr. Fonrose does not dwell on the era in which he grew up or the personal circumstances that forged his character. For him, that was not the point of his writing. His was simply a personal effort to capture memories evoked from photographs he had collected over the years. It is up to you, the reader, to appreciate the times in which he grew to be a man and the challenges of becoming a board certified doctor.

He made no excuses for himself along his journey and always kept his bar high for the standards he set for himself. His formative years were marked with some sadness and separation—the death of his mother at a young and impressionable age, leaving his immediate family and the familiar surroundings of home, his transplant from the urban environment of Brooklyn to the tropics of the humble home of his paternal grandmother in Trinidad. He made the adjustment in stride. Under the care and watchful, no-nonsense discipline of his grandmother, aunt and uncle, he was deeply imprinted with a sense of self-sufficiency and work ethic. Education was highly valued by his family and he was sent to the best school on the island that his family could afford.

Returning to the United States and completing his service in the Navy, Dr. Fonrose locked and loaded on a vision to become a board certified medical practitioner—a vision his late mother had planted in him early as a young child. Armed only with discipline and determination, Dr. Fonrose struck out along this long and lonely path with little support, encouragement, or financial wherewithal. The journey to becoming a doctor is arduous in and of itself. Compound that effort with that of being a black man of meager means in the early 1960s having to run the gauntlet of a medical board in Birmingham, Alabama at the height of the Civil Rights movement and in the heart of Jim Crow practices.

While Dr. Fonrose's purpose is to chronicle his memories over his life's journey, my hope is that you, the reader, will appreciate and take a lesson from a man whose vision and focus enabled him to overcome the personal and societal challenges of his time. Failure to him was not an option. He demonstrated resilience in the face of many obstacles.

I feel blessed that he has long been a part of my family's life—even before my early awareness through my mother—Beryl—who also had a deep respect for his potential and encouraged him to pursue his vision. I respect and admire him for his wisdom and all that he has accomplished over his journey. I thank him for his support and guidance along my journey. I hope you—the reader—can take a lesson from his *"Memory"*.

—Shelley Johnson

PROLOGUE

THE INITIATING IMPULSE FOR THIS project came from a chance viewing of scattered pictures and snapshots, which coincided with the years throughout my journey to express several stages of the passage of time.

Could any or all of them serve as a stimulus or memory to produce a smile, wry or fleeting, or to stimulate an emotion including full-throated laughter on the issue raised? Why not record the event, the memory, the recall that led to this remembrance of things past?

That concept has evolved into a journey—from the past to the present and on to the future.

*   *   *

I was always attracted to the connectability of things to each other, and it explains to me the virtue of chance in addition to merit. The idea of being in the right place at the right time certainly has always appealed to me philosophically; while one can be prepared for something, it seems like there is no force behind it, only the continuity of living.

The timeframe of my journey is divided into four segments to aid description—the formative years, the middle years, the academic years, and the professional years—but each phase is seductively entwined with the former phase, each building on a prior phase, aiding in the integrity of each passing phase.

This desire to maintain a central theme of connectability, memory, and stimuli are stressed and emphasized in *Swann's Way* from *Remembrance of Things Past* by Marcel Proust, which hopefully serves as a template for this narration. In particular, Proust describes the impact of isolated features of his memory to stir up certain occurrences that formed his personality along the way.

Proust's passage, starting with an odor, which was followed by a playful pebble tossed into a stream, is presented as a probe. The tossed rock starts a trail of events on the surface of the stream's water. The initial shock of the contact of the water produces a concurrence of waves and rivulets to both sides of the river banks. Each wave continues with diminishing force and energy to either bank—meeting a dampening force into infinity and unrecognized stillness. And then, is the impulse gone? No! It can only no longer be recognized, thus the end of the energy is embedded.

I believe this episode that Proust describes explains the beginning of who I was and who I have become, and serves as the beginning of the growth of a young man. I think it was the personal recognition that time and energy were not without limits. I'm attracted to the idea that the *end* of it is where I am right now.

It probably is important to point out that Proust was doing this writing during a period of time in Paris, France where the ideas of the French Revolution and the essence of the nature of man were being discussed by several people, Marcel Proust being one of them.

He exposed some of his sociological ideas which turned out to be part of the human contract (or what I call a social contract) which I think was the essence of the ideas that led to the rise of the individual in the 17th or 18th century, as opposed to the Renaissance dark ages in the 14th and 15th century.

So I think Marcel Proust's idea of consciousness and his positive attitudes about the importance of people and the whole social environment was significant and has become the basis of this whole endeavor of remembering my life experiences.

* * *

The idea that each thing connects to each thing, and each molecule attaches to another molecule, which eventually ends up as a total organism, describes the whole concept of integration of things to each other and runs through all of the diagnostic and therapeutic scales of medical thought. This is true not only if we are talking about medicine, but also when we are talking about politics. The fact that this idea also ends up in social thought is no paradox. There's no contradiction.

Any stimulus, connecting to both the past and the future, has a powerful message of memory. Each impulse creates another memory such that recall—initial and distinct and sometimes forceful—can become remote yet powerful so that although unclear at onset, remains vivid and decisive on recall.

Memory as a fleeting embedded emotion, whether it rests on the surface or is deeper, is open to conjecture. The stimulus discharges memory, pleasant or noxious, but is valid and inherent to the human experience.

As the past unfolds, feelings are revealed through memory, recall or stimulus. Some are relevant, some not, but all valid with respect to the past. And again, some may be pleasant (some more so than others). Some foci are easily recalled, while some may be submerged or stilled. Relevance may be revealed by the power of the stimulus. The recall may be vague or it can be clear and pleasantly warming.

But the sensation of all things experienced may be viewed as connected—idea to idea, fact to fact, sensation to sensation—constantly communicating through memory and stimuli.

These moments are all touching and part of a whole. They are still separate and distinct, yet all valid with varying degrees of impact. Thus, the impact of any stimulus on recall and memory could serve as an initiating point of entry to the future.

Usually, but not necessarily, a specific act could focus on a moment. Therefore, it may be appropriate to seek association as an avenue to clarify or explain a pattern of sustained activity. As such, it may be possible to identify the moment that produced that pattern; therefore, my formative years or early years could clarify some literary exercise. But it was early on and indistinct, so it is difficult to ascertain the exact time that the pattern emerged or began. Certainly it was during the middle years when the exposure to the ideas of Proust's literature seemed a better starting point.

An essential plan or stimulus, again toxic or pleasant, could also serve as a focal starting point; it's facile to choose *Swann's Way* in *Remembrance of Things Past* as that seminal event. Perhaps it's *too* convenient to assign all that reading in the middle years such a role of importance but it's where *my* memory of recall evolved as a point of construction.

The impact of certain stimuli started with a most startling recollection of my arrival in Trinidad as a young boy with my sister, Lillian (who I will refer to as Baby Doll in my narrative) in 1935. This one stimulus was the starting point for all that followed in the formative years. But even in hindsight, it's recognizable that the arrival at the four-room house in Trinidad still precipitates a smile upon remembering!

What followed were events of purposeful work and education on my central attitudes and beliefs—which evolved into my current attitudes, judgments, and ethics. Together with sensations of joy and fear, and the processes of defense or survival, these persist to the present and have served through a lifetime of passage from childhood, adolescence and maturation to the adult "performances", both personal and professional.

This pattern of defense, discipline, motivation and purpose have fused into formative function, all of which come from associations with friends, family, playmates and from both losing or winning and adjusting emotions to a changing environment to produce kernels of growth in the formative or early years.

*   *   *

Many distinct works of literature are an important part of this narrative, all pertinent and relating to the flow of any human activity. They express ideas of motion, memory, recall and stimuli, all in constant ebb and flow.

The fact that *it,* meaning the role of memory, could serve as a template of an autobiography seemed valid. A journey of 70+ years flowing from the arrival in Trinidad in 1935 seemed an attractive starting point. The theme would be tested!

The initiating basis of the project and its validity is in confluence with the thoughts of Proust, which appear increasingly valid in the background ideas of motion, stimuli, memory, echo, timing and opportunity. Their accuracy and endurance exist through all of these phases of my formative years, middle years and on into the academic and professional years. Yes! As time moved upon time, the validation seemed only to increase, especially looking back on the formative years from 1935 to 1946.

As events flow and memories unfold, an indistinct or remote collection of stimuli or recall, echoes and impulses that may be stilled, are all waiting for an appropriate time or event to someday bare themselves and create a subliminal or powerful effect. Depending on the depth that separates surface awareness from a deep state of consciousness, our memories may be muted, or they may create an emotional explosion. Whatever the response, the validity of its human characteristics prevails since the facts remain that the impulse derives from a human instinct.

However, the surge of memory to the front probably obeys some orderly process. But the process can be modified by the power and number of similar memory types of each at onset or of the circumstances before they were forced to become remote. This is either by choice or loss of the initiating power of the impulse in the first instance. The power of the energy plus the amount of the memories at onset, before flattening out into infinity, may be the defining issue of the recall process.

That imagery is my mindset for the theoretical years of this memory-touched journey and is the main focus of the narrative following the years from Trinidad to retirement.

The phases as defined—formative, middle, academic, and professional—fit with the template of *Swann's Way* in *Remembrance of Things Past* which also uses memory and stimulation as the mechanisms to illustrate the project's obscure emotion.

The proposition at onset must be conceded in this formulation that memories can and do exist at reference, probably touching each other at three points—before, during, and after an emotion. Therefore, the emotion of arousal emits memory for adjoining memory or recall in any resonating form. That form may be an echo or a sound, which could be mired in thought and expressed as an idea, each touching.

Therefore all events, remote or current, may emerge on stimulation. Sometimes they can emerge as an emotion or a wry smile. The type of response may relate entirely to the first cause. The issue may well be the degree to which the adjacent positioning is a valid assumption.

It seemed reasonable as the test proceeded in this narrative. Similarly, thinking of the concept of chance as suggested in the theme of the novel *War and Peace* by Tolstoy, I decided to test the dialogue of change, opportunity, and timing in a biological sketch so the narrative may begin in the concept of continuity and should continue to sustain the idea throughout to establish its validity. I expect the concepts to be well-demonstrated as the events unfold from a background of memory—silent and submerged and vague.

But any residual sensation probably can be revealed with sufficient force, power, or energy to unify everything experienced as a continuum of ideas. The initiation can be interpreted as a probe, accepting the proposition of the intrinsic validity of memory. The presumption of the adjacency of fact to fact, or idea to idea, would not be unlike a positioning of sensation to sensation.

Then, memory and stimuli merge to connect moment to moment, further accepting the premise of the individual integrity or identity, each as part of the whole mass of memory in a particular engagement. The varying degree of their power and energy emerge on command.

The process may be judged explosive. A powerful enough probe or stimulus, starting as a force with motion and volume, with time and space produces an effect of power, volume, and energy. Yet as each stimulus is dampened by time, it may lapse into stillness. Although it may appear as inactive, truly it may be embedded, waiting for a new energizing force.

The context of Proust's life may be considered lost. But in a human insight of memory, it is not lost, but probably better understood as embedded in some unrealized place! This concept in my judgment can serve a valid purpose in the ruminations as described in the journey that follows.

The narration begins with my arrival in Trinidad in 1935.

THE JOURNEY

THE FORMATIVE YEARS

✳ ✳ ✳

THE EVENTS WHICH LED TO a ten-year stay in Trinidad began with the untimely death of my mother in 1932. Two young children, ages seven and five, were left with the need for continued care and supervision. A young father and bereaved husband was left facing an unwelcome chore. A maternal grandmother was left facing the loss of a favorite daughter.

Some of the early solutions involved spending alternating weekends in New York City and Brooklyn with my father. This placed more stress and involvement on the continued care of the children, which was of paramount focus and importance. All involved were grieving. The financial and logistical stresses are obvious.

My father's early remarriage was a temporary solution but hardly positive. In the angst of that environment, an attempt at a permanent stay in New York City seemed only to increase tension in both households. Perhaps the children became pawns in the interfamily discord. The solution of sending us to my paternal grandmother and her triad of family seemed attractive, thus the decision for transfer to Trinidad. The net result from this perspective seems wise, although that was hardly the view of my maternal grandmother and her family circle.

My father's decision was one I look back upon with some doubt, but for the children was singular and positive. From my personal viewpoint, transferring our care to Trinidad is a major and intrinsic episode as events unfold and fulfills several of the themes that emerge in the rest of the journey. The critical features of that decision to go to Trinidad became integral to all that followed. The flow of events with its relationship to the past, present, and future can hardly be denied.

* * *

Even on repeated review, the full basis of the eventual move to Trinidad rests *entirely* on the untimely death of my mother in 1932.

That sad event produced a trifecta of social needs for solution—(A) continued care of two children at ages seven and five; (B) the need falling fully on the bereaved father of the children; and (C) the grief suddenly descending on the maternal grandmother and her family.

The change of venues appears highly constructive in retrospect and in the tunnel vision of revision. That combination began its motion to the future and the formative years in Trinidad from 1935-1946. Full disclosure requires a peek at the beginning of an adventure that was a trifle untidy.

*   *   *

The sending of two young children on a voyage on the high seas unattended now would be considered an adventure, but was not that easy for a single father of thirty-five years old. I don't think he considered it romantic, and he probably received major criticisms from his in-law's family. His solution involved obtaining an accompanying guardian to serve as a supervising companion for the trip. The fact that his plan succeeded is another testimony to the role of chance and opportunity, not to mention the high degree of fortune and luck.

The seven-day voyage went smoothly and without mishap. The ship's crew banded together and delivered my sister and myself in good shape to Port of Spain where I can still smell the aroma that will be described later in this narrative. However, memory and recall reveal an event which made a mark on my present personality.

During the passage, there was a tendency for the crew to try and entertain the passengers. One episode touched this seven year old boy. There was a two-bag race which I won, but then I refused to enter a contest which consisted of eating blueberry pie with my hands tied behind my back. That picture of eating that pie with hands unavailable and without utensils was an image that filled me with a sense of awkwardness. My refusal to participate under the rules outlined caused unwelcome friction, but I remained adamant. The memory of my refusal remains clear. Personally that attitude resonates to this day on embarrassing interludes and my refusal to participate in unwelcome imagery.

In contrast, Baby Doll remembers the trip vividly because it was the first time she ever ate tomato soup—and she ate it exclusively every evening for dinner during the entire trip from New York to Port of Spain. To this day, her favorite vegetable remains a tomato in any form.

*   *   *

My father had planned well, but he could not have known (and the steamship line must have been unaware) that at the disembarkation point a fee or excise tax in the Caribbean island was a necessary practice.

We were not prepared for that contingency of $100.00 per person. On arrival we did not know why we were left in a room while other passengers were leaving the ship. Eventually we were informed by a member of the staff in Port of Spain.

Fortunately, a fellow passenger by the name of Mr. Cadiz (what memory that I would remember him by name approximately 70 years past!) had become friendly with the young lady who had been hired by my father to keep a watchful eye on us during the seven-day voyage. She had left the ship at an earlier island and had probably asked Mr. Cadiz to observe us on our way to our family in Port of Spain, Trinidad. Whatever the reason, it fell on him to solve this disembarkation problem which he did in gracious fashion.

Mr. Cadiz had a very forceful personality and I remember him as being very well-groomed with an imposing stature that reflected a certain air of confidence. He accompanied Baby Doll and myself to our destination at Four Roads in Trinidad for our safe deposit. It is my best recollection that the $200 loan was satisfied by my father on Mr. Cadiz's return to New York City. I don't recall ever seeing Mr. Cadiz again, although my sister believes he did visit us in Four Roads on one occasion. This is just one memory of the multiple examples of humanity and how it is expressed casually and without notice.

*   *   *

I remember arriving in Trinidad on a sunny morning, and when we got off of the ship, I smelled the aroma which even right now I can recall as a powerful stimulus relating to my years there.

As I think back now, it is probably true that these sensations were mostly from the many mango trees that were on the property. The aroma of ripe mangoes remains part of every thought and memory of my years in Trinidad.

*   *   *

I also remember riding down from the dock at Port of Spain to Four Roads where I would live. I was overwhelmed by the appearance of the house as I arrived. It was a wooden frame home with four rooms. One was immediately on the left side of the house with the bedrooms on the right side of the house. It was built on approximately a half acre with the house in the center of the lot, surrounded by dirt with plenty of room for games or cricket and soccer with boys my age.

There was an outdoor kitchen in the back with galvanized roofing and an earthen fireplace and oven. That area led out to many trees such as mango, orange, and cocoa, all of which contributed to that aroma which my recall has provided. I remember there was an orange tree to the left side of the house and I recall climbing the tree carrying a knife and picking the oranges out.

Frankly, in the period of time when I was about age ten until I was about thirteen years old, my carbohydrate metabolism must've been very high because I would go up into the tree with that knife and just feast myself on a load of the oranges, the peels of which I'd drop to the ground. I remember my grandmother berating me for leaving all of the orange peelings behind. Now I look back at that with a certain sense of pleasantness.

Also in the back of the house were the outdoor latrine facilities which represented the rural aspect of the time and place of the social function of the British and Spanish communities of that period in the early 1900s that is still part of the social fabric.

* * *

Further recollections relate to the roads that went down from Port of Spain to Four Roads. It's interesting that I never thought about why the place was called Four Roads, but in retrospect there were four roads coming together at a point from four different directions of the island.

Four Roads is a descriptive memory. The name and the statement are at the endpoint of arrival by mechanical railroad car which was subsequently updated to electric railroad car. The intersection was at a four-staged gas station, whose central bar served as a gathering place at the corner and as a backdrop to a constabulary station upon and above a crest of an expansive savannah, which served as a playground for cricket and soccer matches on both Saturday and Sunday evenings. On reflection, it was an imposing structure that worked into the Four Roads culture of my association of the four connecting roads and the terminal.

* * *

Foremost on the day of arrival in Trinidad was the focus on my paternal grandmother, Amant (Morris) Fonrose, who from that early moment always remained the dominant figure of my stay of more than ten years. My memories of her are both general and specific. The specific is powerful and can be reflected in events or passages of recall.

For instance, an eye injury occurred during a game of war wherein objects were thrown. One late afternoon, a ripened lemon struck me hard in the right eye. My childish response was to crawl into bed to hide. The next day came forth as it must, and the injury was obviously exposed in the morning sun. The expression on my grandmother's face of tenderness and caring represents the full measure of all that she gave me in those early years.

Another example of her compassion was her habit of welcoming me during a time where I left school and was unsuccessfully seeking a job in Trinidad. This went on for approximately six months without success, and upon my arrival back in Four Roads she was always there with a question, "Harold, how was your day?" The tender concern of her question served as a soothing agent beyond what I can express. It was just a welcome measure of compassion—very welcome—from the daily defeat from which I obviously recovered.

My permanent vision of her is that of her waving on the day of departure from Trinidad to New York as I began the adventure of becoming a physician. What a gallant and graceful person.

*   *   *

Then there was my Aunt Liz, my father's sister, a towering image of strength and steadfastness, always there and ready to solve the multitude of problems coming from the sudden transfer of the responsibility of two children to the island experience. She assumed a central disciplinary role that was both benign but with authority. On any of her visits from the south area of the island, she would arrive with a magical ability to fix and adjust for the comfort of myself and Baby Doll.

In particular, I remember her constant and recurring presence at certain times of celebration or special events. Her visits from an area of the south of the island were numerous and usually salutary. Of special note was her visit at Christmas time. The stripping and cleaning in preparation for holiday practices of an open house in the village community involved layers of work and diligence, which included my grandmother and the children in the household.

Aunt Liz's continued presence was integral to the completion of this process and cannot be overstated. The end product of sparkling glasses and light fixtures in crockery were exposed as if by magic as part of her presence. In addition, her energy in the baking of bread and cakes and cookery was manifested during the Christmas season and made for a joyous intervals marked by her presence. The contribution of her visits and earthy joy was and is part of the memory of things past. In looking back, it is no mystery that her guidance in those early years rendered a foundation for the upcoming future for which I am so proud and pleased.

Aunt Liz's role is well-defined. Her function and determination was central to the development and future conduct of her niece and nephew while in her care.

In later years, after Baby Doll and I returned to the United States, her responsibility became taking care of her mother (my grandmother) who died within two years after our departure. She then assumed the role of caretaker of the house where I spent my years in Trinidad. Aunt Liz, who had never before been employed, worked as a hospital worker in Port of Spain, Trinidad and endeavored not only to care for herself, but to also rebuild the house of her mother. This enabled her to start repairs and add plumbing, water, and acceptable kitchen facilities. Fortunately, her timing coincided with the completion of my medical training. Therefore, my financial contributions to her were very helpful in her rebuilding the house. My wife and I visited Trinidad in the 1965-1970 timeframe and stayed at her home. I also returned in the 1970s for Aunt Liz's funeral and again stayed at the family home.

*　　*　　*

Finally, the rest of the threesome was Uncle Cornel, my father's brother, who was a young man who made his living as a tourist guide. My recall about him is striking—always being immaculately dressed with an easy-going personality. Specifically, I remember when he was a guide for Errol Flynn, the famous actor, and the fuss generated as my uncle drove him around the island. That was a famous celebrity memory.

Uncle Cornel's financial contributions made my education possible outside the boundary of Four Roads at Tranquility High School. He would supply $1.20 per month for my school fees which he earned actively in his role as a chauffeur. There is recall of my need to often wait for his accumulation of the fee, which sometimes would take hours for him to earn. The monthly tuition of $1.20 was both monumental and of overwhelming importance. This well illustrates the real status of economic activity of the island. It also illustrates the magnitude of his contribution and what it came to mean in my development on the topics of algebra, English and philosophy, all of which prepared me for college and the future. Without that offering, there would not be a Harold Fonrose today. No question—that is no overstatement. It is impossible to overestimate his role and the help that it provided in the years that followed in the United States.

*   *   *

It was my distinct pleasure to have entertained both Aunt Liz and Uncle Cornel in my home, separately, in Jericho, New York during the 1970-1990 timeframe. Uncle Cornel visited after the death of his sister. Aunt Liz visited the United States following the completion of the house. Obviously her stay with my family for approximately two weeks was of special significance to her. My wife, Betty, showed her most of the New York sites. Her appreciation of "all of America," as New York was thought of by her, was expressed with her customary dignity and grace.

Memories allow me a sense of satisfaction, gratitude and fulfillment, particularly in 1968 (the exact date is beyond my recall). My wife and I took a vacation to Trinidad. At the Piarco Airport, my proud uncle welcomed me back to the island as a returning physician where the germinal aspects of an aspiring young male started the mission. The description of our meeting with the abundance of pride and esteem can be imagined but only marginally felt if you were not one of the participants. The 40-mile journey was traveled in his taxi, which was old but dignified. By my knowledge of the islands, culture and habits, it made me aware that his taxi was unlikely to produce wild-eyed approval by average visitors. Since his vocation was that of a tourist escort with vehicle, there was no mystery that his economical survival was at risk. Because of his sense of pride, my uncle never asked for anything.

Later, it was my distinct privilege and honor to offer my uncle my enduring gratitude for his gesture to me during my early days at Tranquility High School. Thanking him in the only way that occurred to me. It became possible to have a new Ford vehicle transferred to him. The car had to be a right-handed drive, motor, of English vintage, and the only possible outlet was Canada. Luckily, the Ford Motor Company had an outlet in Canada and by that time I had established a business contact at Ford, as I had owned several of their vehicles over the years. I was able to use the impression of value that could be satisfied and thus aid Uncle Cornel. The car was delivered to him in Port of Spain, Trinidad. An excise tax of approximately $900.00 had to be paid first, which a local bank in the United States was happy to facilitate.

An intervening by-product of the above transaction is offered as a commentary on pride and gratitude. It was on a visit to Trinidad on the occasion of Aunt Liz's death. Upon my arrival, my uncle took me to a local tourist-type hotel for my registration where there was a group of taxi drivers. Upon my introduction by Uncle Cornel to his friends, there was an exclamation of, "Oh, you are Cornel's physician nephew he so frequently cites about his new car which was sent to him. Everybody in Trinidad knows you and that bright yellow car and your generous gift!"

Uncle Cornel had dinner with me that night. That dinner was an obvious glorious episode. My Uncle Cornel was one proud guy.

*   *   *

The combination of the threesome and their influence thereafter began. The recall of the stately, graceful grandmother in the focus of Four Roads is and was prominent. There were lessons on observations—forceful and with enduring stability. Several instances of her serenity and remarkable concern for the welfare of her grandchildren were clear. Her caring came without the sense of having to earn it.

I remember her constant uplifting stature and an utter refusal on her part to look down while walking along the paved road. Her feet would seek the joining of the roadway and the dirt/grass to provide her with the orientation on her path. Grandma was probably legally blind, only able to discern the idea of motion or images. I remember how she would occasionally reach out plaintively with her hands and ask, "Harold, is there a car coming?" Or she would ask for help identifying any one of her friends that had called out to her.

In general, however, it was the force of her presence and her steadfast determination to survive in her reality that forces the vision of her memory. That combination of quiet elegance, grace, and power provided the foundation of my formative years. The ideas of formative and foundation could be used interchangeably because the foundation was carried forth onto the middle years and thereafter.

*   *   *

During the ten-year stay in Trinidad, males and females were treated quite differently, probably reflecting that attitude of the times. I recall that approach was reflected in my grandmother's attitude as I grew to an assumption of maturity. My sister was less involved. There's an easy explanation of either her being of the opposite sex or of different patterns of behavior. Probably both. Baby Doll's experience was similar to that of females in the age group of ten to twenty years of age. I recall a special type of protection directed at her. When she became a teenager, "letters of intent" were presented to her as part of dating and courtship of the time.

Some of the separations of chores between the sexes were reflected in my embarrassment and near shame when on occasion I had forced my grandmother to take on my role of obtaining drinking water on a daily basis to our home. In some way, I had exposed my grandmother to a chore that was beyond her natural role. My sister could not, and indeed should not, be forced into that unseemly role. This is one of those understated aspects of human behavior that had become acceptable and without question.

I do not feel, however, that every difference afforded me was not matched by some responsibility for males and a possible attitude for girls. My ten years was spent as described. Hers were more typical of the attitude and culture and habit that at that time prevailed in the period of 1930-1940. It was unfortunately the way of the world at that time. There was no change until the 1970s. All of these memories were embedded in some unrecognized place. Honestly, it was only recently that my sister, Baby Doll, referred to my favored place in the activity and responses of my grandmother, Aunt Liz and Uncle Cornel. It was exposed in her recall that I was treated differently. I did not challenge her for a second. It's so easy to look at the past moments and assign personal interpretations whether real or imagined. Remote memory, though useful, can be deceptive. Certitude can be a trap which I prefer to avoid when possible! Likewise, simple statements devoid of content can be just too easy and glib.

There is a certain tinge to her conversations with my grandmother and Aunt Liz that speaks volumes of the attitudes, behavior and guidance of the young girls in Trinidad in 1935-1940 as opposed to young males. These differences in my opinion are revealing as a cultural affect and part of the social fabric.

*　　*　　*

I continue on to the present as each layer unfolds and the memories nudge each other. Because of the unfolding, the value of the formative years and their impact seem to increase in reference and cause me to reemphasize their total importance.

The mystery of the power of those formative years and their lasting effect continues to unfold in the family circle of three that provided a just framework for my life which was thrust upon them by my father and his response to the vagaries of human events. There is a sense of personal satisfaction in this recognition of the value and their memory.

The contribution to the notion of formative years as an overall positive experience cannot in my opinion be overstated in my reference to character formation and sensation of confidence that emanates from the ten-year stay in Trinidad.

*　　*　　*

There were several instances of traveling to the local post office to get mail from my father back in the United States. This memory points to his contact with us during the years 1935-1940, along with the major impact of his decision to have care rendered by his mother and his siblings. The toll on his life during that period must have been immense. The economics of the time were well-recorded as part of the Depression. His job was as a chauffeur for a family in Rhode Island, which provided for his economic existence. His contact was maintained fully with near-monthly letters. Not infrequently, some of the envelopes would be marked with red, white and blue borders indicating air-mail transmission. Ha! Those letters from our father usually were filled with money orders of various amounts consistent with his economic state at the moment. Regardless of that particular state, air-mail letters at Christmastime were bountiful and made for recollections consistent with the timely arrival of Aunt Liz. We were never abandoned. If he could not send money, he always kept in contact with us as a father.

There were other times when I could still hear my Grandmother request that I visit the post office to see whether my father had written.

In retrospect, it is clear his role as father and provider was well-honored as part of his persona. Upon my return to the United States, I never discussed that with him as it is now expressed. It is my particular hope that my progress in the middle and later years filled him with a sense of pride and accomplishment which he justly deserved. I never discussed the positive aspects of his contributions with him before his death and I am truly sorry for that.

Asserting the idea of personal privilege, my memory *does* touch on the generational aspects of the preceding discussion and *does* relate to the passage of time of the middle and academic years, using the generational support as a focal point of memories in the background.

In the musings of the past, there was also the history that my father had journeyed to the United States in 1922 to join his father, Charlie, and intended to pursue a career in medicine at his request. These musings silently discussed the loss of that mission after he met my mother. What role my presence played in that decision can only be played out in the course of human memory and history.

*　　*　　*

There is a feature of the early formative years that needs exploration. It is a wooden schoolhouse with outdoor classes and slates. It may be useful to fully describe the Four Road Government School as a way to explore the status or limitations of the educational system in that though rich in rhetoric, history, reading, geography and basic mathematical skills, clearly was marginal in matters of science, physics, chemistry and the like. This would be illustrated in my years of college preparation.

The school almost by definition was a single room, separated into first through seventh grades. Several classes were presented outdoors, usually with books or readers provided. Paper was sparse and expensive. Learning and teaching was hands-on, personal, and up-close. It was easy to both judge and be judged. Learning was a direct discipline, occasionally severe but productive in retrospect. Learning was both an option and a prize. Personal progress was salutary and satisfying. Measuring that progress was monitored weekly and monthly. In retrospect, it is no mystery that my journey was always in comparison to a standard that would clearly be welcome in the competition that followed through the many vagaries of the passing years that were waiting in the future.

*   *   *

There is no recall that suggests any sense of romanticism. Poverty was rampant but we managed to escape the sense of "the poor." All our needs were met so that the derivatives of learning, education, and discipline with ethics were delivered and received. These issues were never considered mundane in the formation period and have been glibly referred to as the formative years.

Some of the self-imposed structure and discipline were probably called out by simple but necessary chores, involved in day-to-day living. Clean water was an obvious priority for food and drinking. As mentioned earlier, it was my responsibility through those early years to deliver buckets of water on a daily basis in a distance of approximately one-quarter mile from a common water source. When the chore was missed (by self-design or by accident), it still remained the priority. I have the awful memory of my stately grandmother filling in on such a chore that I avoided in playful carelessness.

Trinidad was romanticism mixed with reality. But as previously asserted, this structure was the template for the ethical and disciplined behavior which could later be recorded as a positive formulation. Thus memory, mixed with poverty, chores, and responsibility, as valued through a child's eye was fondly stirred in the background of useful, philosophical alternatives. And so, memory and timing fused through conscious thought and maturation to a higher place of behavior and adult formation at the present and future period.

This part of the narrative probably drips with sentimentality but expressing gratitude does seem appropriate and level in the mirror of time. There was worthy activity then in a remote part of the world!

*   *   *

My stay in Trinidad contained a mixture of things including sports, especially cricket. I played with a passion which has been reproduced but never really achieved. There is a picture of me as a young boy—I couldn't have been more than about thirteen years old—playing 2nd class cricket in Trinidad and winning a trophy as a group of young teenagers. We were very pleased with ourselves. The picture shows me in short pants playing a game which I had come to love and played fairly well at this certain time. It is important to recognize that there *is* such a picture and I've looked at it with both a sense of pride and wonderment about what was going on in my mind at that age.

Then there was my education, including studies of some of the classics, and a close intellectual association with George Frederick. George was from Grenada, one of the local islands. He was transferred to Tranquility, the Four Roads Government School, as a teacher so that he could play cricket in Trinidad, thus making him eligible to play on the team which could be selected on the basis of merit to go to England, which would be a great achievement on his part.

He became a very significant person in my life because in my mind he achieved not only that of a teacher but of a strong personality. He was not a father figure, but he certainly helped form my philosophy and attitudes and influenced the basis of who I was and who I became. He took me under his wing as my tutor and taught me algebra and gave me a certain feel for the French language (because as I recall he was fluent in French), but in addition to that, he brought an overview to this young boy. He was a grown young man at that time—about twenty-two or twenty-three years old—with the prestige of being a famous cricketer, and I remember listening to just about everything he had to say with a sense of wonderment.

It is important to recognize that George Frederick had become such a philosophical source in my mind that it was not until my first visit back to Trinidad in 1965 as a physician that I met with him and realized who George Frederick was and who Harold Fonrose had become. It wasn't so much that *he* overpowered me as it was that his *ideas* overpowered mine. The force of his ideas was so important that it created my thinking about several issues of the day as a young boy floating around in Trinidad in the 1930s.

There was a period of time between 1941-1945 when WWII was being fought. American soldiers were in Trinidad at the Chaguaramas Naval Base by the mid-1940s. Suffice it to say, I absorbed his ideas about politics, his ideas about religion, and his ideas about general sociological issues at that time. As he became my tutor, it was a long time before I was able to develop a political and social attitude that was independently mine, perhaps beginning from where he left off.

But the net result is that the influences that he provided when I was a boy between the ages of ten and twenty were if not overwhelming, certainly were very important as to how I behaved as a undergraduate student, a graduate student, a physician, and finally, a father and husband. George Frederick was a very important person in my life at that time.

It is important to realize as I'm talking about it right now that at each stage in my life, starting in the formative years when I identify my grandmother, George Frederick and continuing on through all the following phases of my life, I always met a tutor or a benefactor who would become very, very instrumental in me becoming a physician as the date comes up to the present.

The term foundation in my view actually describes the role of those years of the journey. The stability and the basis of the activity better represent the general purpose of the years that followed in academic and professional activity.

*   *   *

It seems that within a short period following arrival in Four Roads, the theme of musings started in a day by day, month by month dialogue. The musings were of my deceased mother in Brooklyn where this concept or wishfulness that I would become a doctor had its origin. It is not possible to identify, but there it was. In retrospect, I can identify an early tendency defining a future of my return to the United States. As this flowed, there was no urge or prominence, but the thought was ever present and spoke for ambition. The musings and the foundation coincide in the aspect of memory and stability. The notion is focal to this entire narration or journey.

All these obscure memories served as a solid useful base for a full-time day student and part-time/full-time employment in a challenging world. Without that base, and the structural power of the formative foundation, the results may have been negative rather than positive for the progress of those musings. It's all in there, the care and all. Each is connected closely with the preceding and the following period. Each has a separate validity but part of the whole set of events.

The influence of the formative years cannot be overemphasized. Though possible, it is not an option. No mistake here; they were the basis for the future, now realized!

Upon entry into the other world of the United States, striving for the realization of my childhood musings came into focus. The years spent in the maturation process certainly were special, dominant and necessary preparation for the return and the rigorous testing it would provide, rather than the vague echoes of childhood musings. I was well prepared for the coming of the journey. This wonderment as the foundation of the next seventy years is not all that mysterious or accidental. The flow seems natural and expected.

And so, in retrospect, the next step was my return to New York to be rejoined with my maternal grandmother. Timing, chance and opportunity merged, even at this earliest period of my journey. There's a sense of personal gratefulness for the ten-year adventure which led to the preparation for the uncertain future in the United States.

The references to my formative years in Trinidad were always filled with positive, fulfilling events or experiences. There were always discussions of when I would return to the mainland. My deceased mother's musings for my medical occupation education was a distinctive part of formative patterns but the thoughts were exactly that—musings and indistinct echoes of an unsure past.

My presence in Trinidad during the years 1935 to 1945 was somewhat idyllic and filled with the ideas of a teenager in terms of the social endeavors of that Caribbean world. The ticket to New York City, although enticing, brought with it the knowledge of a different world which developed a sense of the unknown. The issue of musing and career will follow in a romantic sense.

The next phase of the cycle came naturally, almost as though it was planned. But it could not have been since the facts did not lend themselves to any known reality that followed in the period 1945-1952. The stimulus was entirely coincident to my birth in Brooklyn. As a U.S. citizen, it became possible to return from Trinidad through the intervention of my maternal grandmother. The use of the phrase intervention may be clarified in the coming description as the reason for the presence in Trinidad as a U.S. citizen for the earlier ten-year period.

*　　*　　*

Presently, my memory of the early years seems to be filled with only positive impulses but the described stimuli can be both positive as well as negative. This brings a wry response because the effort to raise negative impulses was rewarded with some that were rejected. But that restriction was necessary since recall of my arrival in Brooklyn, New York brought out several issues of "the negative" that will provide balance with this narration at the start of the middle years.

THE MIDDLE YEARS

✳ ✳ ✳

I RECALL THE EPISODE WHEN I left my grandmother. It always fills me with a sense of sadness, since I never saw her again after she waved goodbye.

In retrospect, it is welcome to express my regret at the casual tone of my departure that day. That deep regret comes from the thought that my leaving for the airport could have been delayed and could have been a vast and enormous moment. But that was not on my mind in 1946.

That specific moment was in the context of an eager 20-year old male and not my view now as I look back so many years later. The difference of time, place, attitude and general appreciation of self are vastly different and cannot, indeed should not, be transferred one to the other.

The moment passed. The regret is assumed that another moment of delay did not occur. I suspect that the difference of any of the moments at that point in time would have been moot. Further, my regret in not delaying the separation is only part of the moment. My grandmother's view of the separation, though she did not wish it, may have been that she was ready for me to go to that "other world" for which her grandson now yearned.

Yes, the moment passed. Unfortunately she did not have to reflect on regret as I have. I would suspect that she had none, only love. I doubt seriously her fingers would clasp back firmly and not let me go.

My view is an example of experiencing the present fully. My grandmother's entire past, present and future merged into that moment. Any attempt to reinterpret it or apply a greater significance is moot, probably pretentious, and unreal whereas the moment that was lived fully is reflected in the memory of the wave goodbye which I recall vividly with no created apology. Without reservation, I did love my grandmother and her total memory.

Another minute spent with her that day could not change the regret of the day I feel now. It seems this is the true meaning of the "now" and the casual statement is that we really live in the future. This heartfelt apology only emphasizes the futility of backward thinking. But the memory is still valid, with or without the regret. Of course, there is no way to have known that the wave of her hand would remain the moment. Only vague, but I still bear that as part of my memory of my gracious and stately grandmother. Another memory embedded in some undiscovered place. Crying now does not help.

But that episode did prepare me for the measure of emotion I felt during my travel from Trinidad to Brooklyn. The trip from Miami to

New York City in a Jim Crow railroad segregated train was hardly what I expected, and I had no previous experience to use as a defense. Suffice it to say, that was a grossly negative and unwelcome experience.

My only sense of that whole experience was hollow. I was numb. And while I recognize the total indignity of it, I had built into my personality an attitude of acceptance of things as they are.

After boarding the plane in Trinidad, what followed was a 12-hour flight to Cuba, followed by a six-hour layover before flying to Miami. I wore a suit with a white shirt and tie since the standard of the day for travel was to be in full dress. Upon my arrival in Miami, I went to the railroad station to get my train to New York. I was placed in a car directly behind the motor which during the process of the travels emanated occasional bursts of soot and smoke. The natural ending was my white shirt was the same color as the dark suit that I wore as I left Trinidad.

I sat in my train seat—in that one place—for the entire thirty hour ride to New York. During that passage we stopped at several stations along the route for the access of many local people of the Florida communities. There were people who came into the Jim Crow car with chickens, food, and furniture they intended for use at their place of destination.

But I stayed in that seat—straight through—night and day—without moving except for toilet needs. I did not eat. I *would* not eat. I rejected the acceptance of the circumstance by reflecting on the present. That did not change until Washington, D.C. At that time, the conductor "proudly" said, "Now you can come up front." I rejected this attempt at equality. I was not in the mood for any type of cooperation. I sat in that seat the same way I entered it in Miami as if I possessed it.

My arrival at Grand Central Station in the early morning was welcome. I'm sure I was hungry. An uncle, who I had left behind in New York City in 1935, greeted me with a perfunctory, cold and unwelcome gesture and the simply inquiry, "Fonrose?" He could not or did not use my first name of Harold. I have never forgotten how bleak my reception in New York was. Thank goodness for that detached persona.

The same day, I was welcomed by my maternal grandmother's family circle, which provided safety but little else. For some woe-begotten reason, one of my greeting aunts challenged my ambitious assertion of my educational goals. The reality of her arguments on the marginal education received in Trinidad and the meager financial status spoke facts on the reality of the journey and the lack of reality of the plan. This harsh exposure of facts was hardly helpful though true. My initial impressions on arrival remain a constant source of negative impulses. Thus ended the formative years.

*   *   *

That reality of the middle years came fast and furious in the first two weeks following my arrival. Full-time employment was arranged in a furniture store. It was hardly my major choice. A marginal salary saw little relief for maintenance and savings. The financial aspect of my "musings" had a harsh tone of economic severity. But as fortune evolved, options also evolved.

As a returning United States citizen in 1945, I was eligible for the draft. My father inserted himself in both dialogue and discipline. Enlistment became his choice by definition. There was no alternative judgment. Luckily his opinion was decisive and prevailed in the enlistment into the United States Navy, which ensued approximately one month following my departure from Trinidad. The formative and productive middle years fused and became the fruitful cornerstone for the next sixty years to the present.

The overwhelming value and its firm relationship to chance, timing, opportunity, and memory pick up the middle of the journey and characterize the future.

*   *   *

Sometimes transitions can be seamless. Musings and assumptions can be a measure of obscure effects. The cumulative negatives on the way back to the United States as described had a factual basis that should not be ignored. However, these negatives were only impressions as opposed to the positives that had become part of the human pattern derived during the formative or early years. So balance was clearly in my favor.

The facts involved in the navy enlistment were vastly more important in the new period, especially as it relates to the journey and further commentary on the characterizations on *War and Peace* by Tolstoy. Combining issues of remote U.S. citizenship, a persistent intervening maternal grandmother, and the maturation of the ten-year stay in Trinidad, all resonate with *Remembrance of Things Past*. The issue of timing and chance seems clearly demonstrative of this episode.

The transition to the second decade of an idyllic stay in Trinidad, allowing the time to mature, seems preordained to aid in the rigors of student life and hard work, to match the sustained ambition.

All of these aids were going to be necessary to supplant "the musings" of a deceased parent. So much for destiny! Again, the transfer of want and desire to the United States led to an important variation on destiny or chance.

*   *   *

As previously suggested, the draft still being possible in March of 1946 required a decision. Enlistment in the Naval Hospital Corps became the option of choice. The intention was to try for the role of pharmacist mate. The possibility of assuming that status had only recently become available. In timely fashion, President Truman by Executive Order had opened all lines of service for American black citizens. Prior to this, my only recourse in the navy would have been off-line duty in the kitchen-service division. Entry to hospital corps school was achieved in Portsmouth, Virginia—the next stop on the way to training for a pharmacist mate and/or nursing aide.

This reality had an intriguing by-play with my father. It's relevant to remember that the enlistment occurred within one month of my return to the United States. Therefore, my father's advice to enlist registered as "his" and my personal sacrifice. This firm paternal advice to volunteer was tested to the core.

The act of the enlistment which my father witnessed at the front of the Enlistment Office, was followed approximately eight hours later with him still waiting there for my return at that front entrance. As the accompanying group sailed by, someone advised him, "He's in the Navy now on his way to boot camp for six weeks of training." He was aghast at the finality of the episode. Reluctantly, the full recognition of his advice had come forth. The look on his surprised face clearly fulfills the idea of a remembrance.

My own emotion, though subdued, was no less astonished. But I think my formative years stood fast on the issue of the acceptance of the facts as they were presented. In retrospect, it's clear I was prepared for this unhappy eventuality. Suffice it to say, I survived boot camp.

My two-year enlistment, which was decreased to twenty-two months by the President's decree, was a wholesome and valuable interlude which was integral to the rest of the journey and events that evolved.

* * *

The completion of the six-week stay in boot camp is followed by orientation to the armed forces of the navy. The next step for the role of a pharmacist mate was entry into the hospital corps school for six weeks during which adequate theoretical and practical features of the duties of a pharmacist's mate would be explored. Subjects of study and practical procedures of nursing care were delivered in structured class work. Routine testing in areas of learning was a base requirement. The relative success was routinely rewarded with expectant leave or liberty in the adjacent city of Norfolk, Virginia. Liberty was awarded as a token for interval success.

On one occasion I went into the local Norfolk region for some entertainment with certain members of the corps school. Unknowingly we had entered that part of the U.S. where southern attitudes on race and religion ruled. The visit was unpleasant. I never tried that privilege again. Members of my hospital corps class with northern attitudes and orientation had offered protection but I could not, indeed would not, experience a replay of the Civil War. I stayed put on the hospital corps grounds for the rest of the training. But destiny followed me in another adventure prior to completion of my training for the role of pharmacist mate.

From time to time during corps school, patterns of activity, dress adaptation, and standards of the military required review. On one such occasion, when both personal and general review were involved, the state of my hair needed redress. The naval personnel in charge of such matters came under censure as indeed I did. The issue of an untidy appearance of hair became in contention. My resolute status of not returning to the Norfolk, Virginia area was an issue that required immediate resolution. The base commander issued a direct order that the needs of my appearance could be attended to and be satisfied on base. The net result was the confrontation between culture and military regulations on base over the reluctance of some civilian personnel who only mildly objected due to the order being given. I refer to its resolution as an instance where culture was accommodated and an easy solution was found.

There was another episode during the time when I refused to accept off campus liberty. It was about mid-day and I was with a group of other sailors in Sunday dress. We had stayed on base enjoying our off day and playing some ping pong. We were picked up by someone with authority who saw us relaxing and assigned us to a detail of transporting tubs of meat to and from the storage area to the dining area. It turned out to be one of those instances where my timing and opportunity was off since the group of sailors became involved for approximately twelve hours of hard work that did not end until about 2AM. I'm reminded of it to re-emphasize the penalty obtained for not going off on liberty.

*   *   *

That fortuitous detour through the navy had singular and positive results in every aspect of the journey. One, it served as a preparatory course for my entire medical clinical career. Two, it provided the financial basis for the pre-med collegiate and graduate school integration since the GI Bill offered a one-to-one month relationship for college and graduate school tuition. And three, training as a nursing assistant provided me part-time or full-time employment which was always available to me during the years at Adelphi College and Cornell University studying for my bachelor's and master's degrees.

It's not possible to underestimate how helpful this became since wherever my residence was during those years, part-time work as an orderly or nursing assistant was always in demand. Thus, there was never a period of forced unemployment during the years of preparation.

My constant contact with patient care served in good stead as a student/resident physician. Close-up attention to the sick became a great strength in the hands-on contact with patients in critical care. Bedside performance is a formidable part of the medical art. I fear that this has been lost in the milieu of present data-based or evidence-based care. On every level of the two-year tour in the navy, it was a special and useful aid in forming my final identity. First and foremost, the financial aspects were practically solved, at least for the years 1948-1952.

Further, the educational aspects in medical disciplines were standardized and fairly firm as the basis of awareness derived through the six-week course in the hospital corps school.

Perhaps most important, there was the training as a nurse corpsman which provided the entry to the pragmatic and theoretical aspects of patient care. Following the status where the theoretical implications were given, creating insight into the given areas of medicine, i.e., physiology, anatomy, and mechanisms directly related to medicine, my background was perfect. The attitude was apt and my role as physician was clearly superior in the precious learning years of student, intern, attending and teaching physician and the practical role of directing a medical staff in the final half of my career leading into retirement.

But the most critical part of the passage was the chance meeting of my mentor and major benefactor, Dolie McQuinney Adams. She will be discussed in some detail during the immediate years post-graduation.

*   *   *

The rest of the period of my stay at hospital corps school was uneventful and graduation followed easily. My earnest desire that I need to end up in the top third of the class on merit was achieved. This allowed me to choose a hospital assignment away from the Deep South. I ended up at St. Albans Naval Hospital in Jamaica, New York. But indeed, I was informed that in no event was the navy going to assign me to any hospital other than Boston or New York. Apparently, the navy was well-prepared for any eventuality. I did not know that so I studied hard. Of course, the information and the discipline stood me in good stead as my performance showed in my future academic years.

*   *   *

The physician in charge of my unit at St. Albans Naval Hospital was a resident in neurosurgery. My role was to assist him in several procedures and we worked well together. My contact with him led to his interest in my musings expressing interest in a medical career.

Whatever his motivations, his interest led him to ask me a deliberate and forceful question, "Harold, why do you want to be a doctor?" He then admonished me by saying, "I'd be careful since your response could be critical."

My response *was* careful and deliberate. "I don't think I could ever be bored in the profession." He then arranged for a dinner meeting with his wife and his mother-in-law, Mrs. Dolie McQuinney Adams. Mrs. Adams became a guide, mentor, and benefactor. Of major importance was her community and political contacts of long-standing.

My tour of duty in the navy ended but Dolie McQuinney Adams remained in a sphere of influence throughout my life. I also served as her medical consultant until her death.

The terminal part of the naval career involved preparing for college. There was a need for a high school graduation in New York State, which I could achieve through testing.

The pattern of full-time work at night and daytime school work began in the final six-months in the navy corps. GED equivalence was obtained and supplemented by study at Delehanty Commercial High School. The regents' tests were successful for American history, English literature, and mathematics. They served as the basis for matriculation at Adelphi College in the summer session in 1948 and full course work in September of that year as part of the four-year graduation requirements.

THE ACADEMIC YEARS

THE ACADEMIC YEARS BEGAN SOFTLY, unheralded by any formal announcement. The flow of events as a starting point for its part of the middle years is recognized, but only through the tunnel vision of memories, though far and indistinct and subject to recall on demand.

The practical vagaries in the initial college years involved problems of housing, finance, and travel to school, of which I had no previous experience for my consideration. The freshman and sophomore years at Adelphi were spent in a family household, which was not conducive for a college student's study orientation. The junior and senior years were spent in rental rooms close to the school. The practical consequence was to work full time at night as an orderly. The rigors of off-campus living became a prominent issue; all of the excuses for failure may explain my marginal academic performance. It certainly did not appeal to medical schools, and so the first attempt at admission ended in rejection—with the ratio of applications to rejections approaching levels of forty or fifty to one. Medical school admission would have to wait for the future. There began a period of doubt and indecision, a sense of being alone and loneliness which were not persuasive of any bright future.

The option of attending commencement programs seemed like a charade and an unnecessary challenge. In spite of great reluctance, an invitation by a casual classmate led to my attendance. Chance and timing again seemed my star. The information I learned there was that Cornell School of Nutrition might be an acceptable option for a graduate degree, and a master's degree in nutrition and biochemistry was preferable to accepting that I would not be going on to medical school at all. It was a pleasant experience to apply and be accepted for a two-term program. The preparation for transfer to Cornell University upstate living presented new challenges. Nighttime work as an orderly continued through the summer of 1952.

A sense of continued optimism was now a choice. But in that mix a sense of loneliness emerged in a particularly memorable episode that lends itself to this narrative.

It occurred in December of 1952, when I was in the pattern of working from 11PM until 7AM and suffering from intense stress. The usual pattern began at approximately 9:45PM following a day of schoolwork. On this particular occasion, there was a social event wherein the landlady of my rental room was hosting a Christmas party. My dim but sad recall was of the sound of music and laughter and spontaneous merriment that carried upward to my room.

Upon descent, the host introduced me as her proud tenant and said, "This is Harold, who is on his way to becoming a doctor." That was hardly my mood as I presented on to work in the appropriate garb.

Most devastating however was the gasp, followed by silence upon this disclosure as the tinkle of music and laughter merged. The sense of "What?" followed me as I managed my escape through the door. They could not understand that as a young man I was going to work at a time when everyone else my age was celebrating the holiday. None of this embarrassing anecdote was directed to me, but the memory at that time was a rampant feeling of the futility of the journey, a feeling of desperation. The episode stands out as one of the coarsest of my journey. It remains as a stance of retrospective humility.

*   *   *

This is a fine moment to transition from that indelibly low point back to my memory of arriving at Cornell and a positive future since clearly this step was an improvement and was progressive. Registration for the two-year program in biochemistry and nutrition started in September of 1952.

Being in Ithaca at Cornell is such a pleasant recall that the best description may well be found in the term "wonderment". My presence on the Cornell campus in pursuit of the graduate work was easily beyond my best expectations. The campus at that time had the reputation of being the most striking and picturesque campus in the country. It was easy to be impressed.

The detail of where to live was solved by a mutual friend named Fenton Sands who I met that fall. Fenton helped me in finding a room and housing with the Rucker family.

Fenton influenced my early survival at Cornell. It was the beginning of a two-year program that led to a master's degree in biochemistry. He was already involved in the PhD program at Cornell in the agricultural field of agronomy. He finished his doctorate program and accepted an assignment for agricultural work in Africa for the next ten to twelve years.

Fenton and his wife, Dorothy, always served as a reservoir during my days when food was meager. It is testimony to their sense of compassion that somehow there was always room at the table for me with their family. Without their friendship, the Cornell experience would have been less worthy and certainly without adequate nutrition.

There was a financial burden in renting that was covered by my sister, Baby Doll. She made material contributions to the whole journey, but specifically in this period of time of graduate school at Cornell University during my master's program. Her contribution to my rental housing from 1952-1954 represented a major portion of her earnings during those two years. It could not be overemphasized. It compares favorably with the financial gift of my Uncle Cornel in terms of comparative value, both financially and as a measure of their worth.

The other financial aid came from my benefactor, Dolie McQuinney Adams, following my marriage in 1956. She provided the financial lift needed following entry to my sophomore year in medical school. Until that moment, I had studiously rejected any financial help from her.

*   *   *

Friendships again left an indelible imprint in the middle years seen through the time and events at Adelphi and Cornell. Recall of one in particular that involved a heavy dose of memory has both structure and substance.

At the onset of the college years at Adelphi, my stay with a family in Woodside has a texture of resonance. A firm and casual friendship arose from a park bench discourse. The dialogue spoke reams on ambition and future. I often felt lonely in those years. The fact that there was a ready ear to listen and believe in my ranting for several immature but promising years had an incalculable and positive effect. The fact that she was attractive was a salutary addition. The relationship was intended to validate the ambitions on the reality of the journey at that moment in time.

All of the Socratic discussions with her may have had possible overtones of the personality as rendered in Don Quixote. Quixote was totally idealistic as well as a romantic. I did a lot of talking and had a lot of airy perceptions, most unrealistic in the background of what was true. I had no real chance of becoming a doctor other than my own aspirations. She may have thought me to be an idealistic fool! But at graduation, her inspiration merged with my ambition.

Some of the difficulty with academic work is part of my history. The college years that were endured and the initial shock of rejection at the end of the pre-med years were definitely aided by her philosophical support and the emotional repair that helped me go on to graduation and to continue with night-time employment. This friendship was platonic as so defined. It was an immense outstanding force.

Beryl, the lady of the park bench discussions, and I remained fast friends throughout the path to Cornell graduation and subsequent admission to medical school in 1954.

My wife, Betty, joined the journey and my aloneness was cured. Betty and Beryl became firm friends after our marriage in 1956 and their friendship survived for approximately fifty years. The impact of friendships as a motivating force can be illustrated and germane. The memories continue with input from the families. Here the memories are very close to the surface and can be easily aroused since they were never buried.

*　　*　　*

The basis for the graduate work was in the mechanisms of biochemistry, physiology, and bacteriology. This perfectly suited any pre-med background; however, several of the courses were directed at the pre-med students and served as a winnowing schedule. Presumably, the competition was keen.

My initiation to chemistry caused an early stumble. Contact with the rigors of qualitative analysis produced an unacceptable failure which almost led to curtailing the ambitious journey. In some level of despair, consultation with my faculty advisor in the graduate program, Louise Daniels, proved wise and timely. She insisted that the decision to leave was premature since the failure had been associated with the first test of the semester. From her experience, that first testing was intended to "shock". Another foray into the mid-semester exams was both necessary and worthy.

The issue of timing and chance struck a positive chord. The future unfolded and the next series of exams started in the graduate program providing enough success that the process was completed in 1954. My faculty advisor celebrated my master's thesis on Cholinesterase and Anemia with gusto as she was able to enjoy the results; mindful of my earlier inclination to accept failure too early. Silent cheers to Ms. Daniels and her positive influence and leadership.

The character of this episode is not dissimilar to the interlude of the young woman on the park bench. Both of their votes of confidence were intrinsic to any future success.

*   *   *

Many special contacts on my journey show the force of chance, humanity, and the positive aspects of the *social contract*.

Further, emphasizing these remote memories, there is the central issue of finances and scholarly activity. Of course, employment was necessary and easily obtained in the college infirmary due to my nursing background achieved in the navy, but the day-to-day issue of funding my education and eating on a sustained basis always provided a source of anxiety and/or near deprivation.

A gambit which belies current attitudes on social behavior can be encapsulated in a recurring theme during the two-year stay in Ithaca. There was the process of buying meal tickets for $5.00 worth of food items. It became a known feature of casual humanity that I could make a purchase for 75 cents yet would only be charged 50 cents, which would increase the value of my meal ticket. This practice was well-known and was frequently done by both workers as well as owners of the diner on an on-going basis. Further, Cornell fed college students every Thursday with steaks and chips for $1.00. There were fond memories of value in the experience far beyond the monetary input.

*   *   *

Another singular and memorable gesture was rendered by the owner of the house in which I rented a room on a monthly basis, thanks to my friend, Fenton Sands.

Mrs. Rucker, who frequently would prepare evening snacks for her husband, Henry, would always remember me in their upstairs room immediately at the top of the stairs. It still is almost possible to hear her footsteps on the stairs in late evening inquiring, "Harold, would you care to share the evening hamburger?" In retrospect, I recall it was probably the only acceptable meal I had enjoyed in several days. Usually that left me satisfied for my late night studies.

I'm always impressed with these casual episodes of humility that are expressed at the least expected times. This episode is included since without these incidents, it is unlikely the journey would have had the kind of completion now looked back upon in this retirement reflection.

* * *

So the Cornell experiences proved salutary and meaningful from both an academic departure and the human experience.

The closure of the cycle at Ithaca could be measured on several levels. Except for its impact on my improvement in academic study habits, the memories cited above represent the core of the two-year period. The entire adventure of Cornell had a distinctive similarity to the growth pattern endured in the formative years, especially when viewed from the perspective of the rigors of medical school, internship, residency training, and the progress of board certification, functioning, and attending training programs.

It certainly was instrumental in the interview process, which can be a harrowing experience, and my admission to medical school in 1954. My preparation for my master's thesis on the topic of Cholinesterase and Anemia was very helpful and I was well-prepared after having given several seminars on the topic. When the time came for my interview, my experience was clearly helpful, and I knew it was. It was delivered in telling confidence. The entire memory has a compelling aura.

* * *

Upon my admission to medical school in 1954, there was a particular journey to visit my grandfather in August of that year. Accepting the burden of indistinct memory, my recall is a classic image of my grandfather in the living room of an apartment wherein I told him of my admission to a career that subsequently unfolded. His response was a typical cavalier wave and statement, "Good for you, son." Obviously it was a signal and unforgettable exchange.

There is another satisfactory set of imagery in this tale of generational passing where I had the distinct privilege of playing out the father/son transfer of my graduation from Howard University Medical School in 1958 with a repeat of that image played out with my son, Mark, in 1987. It occurred on the same graduation grounds—25 years apart—almost in the fashion of a passing of the torch. Mark serves as an internist and an ER physician. And so, the generational urge of my grandfather wanting his son to be a doctor is complete with myself and my son, Mark.

My personal privilege for both joy and attribution is hereby acknowledged. I hope the reader of this narration will abide by my enforced humility as I address this issue of grandfather, father, and son.

*   *   *

The summer of 1954 served as a period of financial preparation prior to entry into medical school in September. My summer experience as a full time orderly had preceded my four years at Adelphi, so during the summer of 1954, full days and night-time employment permitted the opportunity to earn full tuition expenses for this freshman at Howard University Medical School. Full disclosure reveals that even the first year was supported by part-time work in the Emergency Chemistry Lab and the Blood Bank. Again, my training activity in the naval hospital corps came to the fore and aided in the historical transition to the present from the past.

*   *   *

The time spent in the initial part of the middle years paid early and late dividends and continued almost surreptitiously.

As previously stated, the preparation endured in the initial training at the navy hospital corps school included basic experience in biochemistry and physiology and was valuable and useful in the first and second years in medical school, a period reserved for gaining the scientific background before starting the clinical experiences of the junior and senior years.

Work as a supplement in the later years continued. The proviso of marriage to Betty in 1956 played a significant role in financial matters. However, two developments intervened to explain away my obstacles to study and complete this phase of the journey.

Academic performance now provided some scholarships—one quarter in my sophomore year and one-half in my senior year. Further, my benefactor Dolie McQuinney Adams provided a monthly stipend starting in the junior year and continued in the years on to graduation.

Positive results continued until graduation in 1958. The academic years of the journey were now complete. Expectant joy was realized and the other half of the project rewarded. The journey was joined by

Betty since she had just completed her master's program at Columbia in Developmental Psychology.

The next station of the tour would be in Los Angeles, California. Westward Ho!

* * *

At this juncture in the journey, my story gets into a more personal tone. The trip to California post-graduation was severe and more of recent vintage.

Obviously there was haste and anxiety for my completion of the trip and arrival in California at Harbor General Hospital for the beginning of the medical journey that has encompassed my life for the past thirty years. The tempo was pregnant with all that transpired following graduation ceremonies and the celebrations of June 6, 1958. Anything which interfered with that objective of starting my internship on July 1st was "in my way."

Betty and I were in Washington D.C. While we could have just embarked for California, the east coast was on the way. With that in mind, we began the trek by car back to New York City. While there, my sister and father and some of my family were joined in the mood.

Following that, there was a stay with the family in Queens where Betty had lived during my last two years at medical school. We did not lounge there long. After a decent but short stay, we eagerly headed west.

All our worldly goods were in that now classic 1956 Chevrolet. On the way, it was helpful to visit some of Betty's family along the New Jersey Turnpike. Free lodging was a requirement. The next leg of the trip was to meet and stay with her Ohio family contingent.

Accepting the concepts of rumination, memories, and the aspect of continuity of emotions and generational flow allows me to invoke another aspect of timing and connectability of events. This one aspect is singular and special.

It is particular in that until that time, I had never met Betty's family, which was immense and protective. Marie, Betty's aunt, had always played the role as a mother for Betty. The visit on the way to California was short in every sense, but they understood my haste to be on my way.

The departing scene of Betty's Aunt Marie waving goodbye is poignant and highly reminiscent of the scene played out with my grandmother when I left Trinidad on my way to New York in 1946. That vision of my grandmother waving as the car departed is fixed in my memory and compares in kind with the departing scene from Ohio on our way to California. The connection is clear and sentimental in Betty departing from her mother-replacement figure and my departure from my mother-replacement figure. The scenes are repetitive and timely, almost to a fault. The evidence is mixed in the concept of memories and is another worthy example to the ideas of both timing and chance.

*   *   *

Again, there was that sense of urgency for "California, here I come!" But the trip would obviously take at least five to six days. It was now the middle of June in 1958.

Our trip evolved into a picnic-like adventure along Route 66. I have a blurry recall of an overnight stay in Chicago. The rest was a lazy-like crawl across the United States that we fondly remember. But there is a lot for newlyweds to discuss—with one of them just graduating from medical school—such as a family and future dreams. We rushed through Arizona and the Grand Canyon, and then on to Las Vegas, which was an unpleasant memory. Black couples were not welcome on the Las Vegas Strip, in spite of the sensational talk of the Rat Pack with Frank Sinatra and Sammy Davis, Jr. Our stay clearly would not be welcome and we rushed on to California, which is what I wanted in any event.

We hurriedly buried our discomfiture and moved on to our primary destination of Los Angeles. Seeing Harbor General Hospital was the first impression of my internship and what could be expected from this brand new physician. Las Vegas be damned!

My first sight of the former naval base, now a hospital surrounded with long-tunneled Quonset barracks was somewhat of a disappointment but allowed musings when I was traveling on those walks—whether slow or fast—along the corridors and interpreting their presence in this internship challenge. A challenge that was suffered by all interns at the beginning of residency training but as the experiences increased, the feelings of doubt subsided into peace. I was never again disappointed with the opportunity for discovery of my medical skills.

The experience of all episodes of a rotating internship was superior and fulfilling. My internship class of thirty-six new physicians was helpful in all areas. The interweaving of the separate medical cultures from all of the other medical colleges was an invaluable perspective as we watched each other in learning and insights. My personal presumption was an immense sense of pride in how my preparation at Howard University easily matched and sometimes surpassed those presented from all over the medical community.

Within a short period of time, the natural fear of performance receded and the learning curve evolved at a predictable rate. It was satisfying to be involved with a discipline that provided comfort and a sense of being well-placed. Timing, chance, and memory had merged in my favor. There were certain clinical episodes where by virtue of memory and performance, habit and steadfastness, the discipline emerged. The rotations through medicine, surgery, pediatrics, and ob-gyn served as a cornerstone upon which the specialty of internal medicine was built. I view the present practice of avoiding internships with a sense of loss and chagrin in terms of the modern vintage of physicians whose residency offers direct entry to the specialty training. It is regrettable, but so be it.

The next cycle came to be the choosing of the site of my specialty training. There's an old adage among venerable physicians that there's wisdom of doing your training in the area where you intend to practice. Sometimes the instincts overlap. The best place is not necessarily the best practice site. There's no more challenging or difficult option, but there is also no preparation for that in the years prior to the decision of where you do your residency. I chose to return to the east.

*   *   *

The preceding discussion touches on two entwining themes. The first is the tendency and desire to prepare for medical performance in the area where there is local knowledge and previous precious experience. That's a powerful impulse. Thus, I chose the return to Nassau County Medical Center, formerly Meadowbrook Hospital, where I was an orderly back in the years 1950-1954. Familiarity is a given for the venue of successful practice of internal medicine. Second, the theme of memory and recall has an emotional and romantic resonance that is inherently powerful and hard to resist. Its relationship to the general theme of this narration exercise should be obvious. Even now, the memory of pursuing my goals in these halls brings forth a wry smile and, "What? I did it!"

Several other reasons could surge on request—some positive, some negative. But as previously cited, any and all of them can be valid in terms of their individual integrity.

Meadowbrook was chosen for residency training and internal medicine and any of the other residency programs recalling me to the region suggested a positive outcome for the practice of medicine. There was early acceptance for return to the New York/Long Island area. I have no regrets. My previous activity as an orderly did not in any way interfere with my present role of resident physician. There were a few tremors in the nursing senior staff but by and large, it was a welcome transition—smooth and celebratory.

The training was unique, general, and thoroughly in tune with coming changes in cardiology, oncology, and nephrology. A renal club was started, of which I was a charter member. There, six months passed, and an autopsy rotation was an invaluable enterprise. It turned out to be singular and one of a kind.

The final years as a senior resident fully in charge of the medical wards under an attending supervisor and chief of medicine and senior attending staff guided me well through the ensuing years of preparation for Board Certification and advancement to Fellowship in the College of Physicians. Eventual management of a medical service in a skilled nursing facility in geriatric care followed.

THE PROFESSIONAL YEARS

✳   ✳   ✳

M Y POST-RESIDENCY PROGRAM WAS VALUABLE and fruitful. Private practice started generally in a pleasant area of Nassau County. My last rotation as a chief resident was helpful and the attending chief under whom all physicians rotate in a supervisory capacity was also beneficial in my preparation for practice in Nassau County. He arranged for my early admission to the medical staff at several of the local institutions. Further, I immediately began admitting patients to my service through his intervention, thereby providing me with an early and fast start to economic survival.

Nevertheless, part-time activity with assured income would be useful and prudent in the presence of a family, now with four sons. Part-time support was sought in two individual areas in those early years of 1962-1963. On one level there was my role as disability consultant in the social security system that in a short time led to a supervisory role. It proved attractive to private insurance companies seeking expertise in disability. The other part-time role as a consultant attending physician in a local geriatric institution also led to supervisory activity, initially as the Assistant Medical Director and finally as the Medical Director from 1971-1986 before retirement.

Board Certification was successful in 1968. The events associated with the passage are special and relate here as only a function of memory—special episodes consistent with themes recited with the prologue. The instance concerns the timing of circumstance and social interplay. My oral interview occurred in Birmingham, Alabama in 1968. The civil rights struggles were going on, but my presence was handily accepted at a local Holiday Inn without incident or controversy. The oral exam was conducted by the department chairman for forty-five minutes. The fact that my performance was equal to that of any consultant in academic medicine heralded a new vision of acceptance for the roles of black physicians. I remain proud of both—the inference and the fact.

In this same perspective, upon my advancement to fellowship in the College of Physicians, one of the Howard University professors who was the chairman of the Department of Medicine was at that time a governor in the college. He happened to be present at the presentation of my advancement to fellowship. There is no greater honor or recognition than to be welcomed as an equal by a former teacher. Thus, I was honored by Dr. Walter Lester Henry, who is now deceased.

The role of the medical director of a geriatric institution was intrinsically responsible for my advancement in the college. The management of that position forced my awareness for teaching some standards. The educational program directed at both physicians and nurses under my responsibility led to lectures and programs that the government board of the College of Physicians agreed were invaluable for the advancement of geriatric care. It was my happy and timely decision to take up that specialty because of the burden soon to be inflicted by the American society in terms of care of the aged. That sentiment was vague in the period 1970-2000 but not any longer. The reality is now. The problem of sustained care of the geriatric population is abundant and clear. I trust some of the disciplines described help in the present and the future.

*   *   *

There have been multiple indistinct references to mentors and benefactors, including Dolie McQuinney Adams. She became a moving force in the journey in the mid-course of the middle years. Her financial aid in the last year of medical school was beyond measurement of value and consistency. In a small effort to demonstrate in her honor, there was my sponsorship of the Dolie McQuinney Adams Rotating Medical School Loan Fund for medical students at Howard University Medical School. The program began with my input in 1972 and remains viable to the present day, as we were so assured by the dean in 2006. Mrs. Adams welcomed the initiative and always publicly praised her sponsorship. I remain indebted to her abundant unselfish humanity.

*   *   *

I always felt an unspecified urge for teaching. The opportunity came early in 1980. Colleges and professional school tuition for the children encouraged me to seek a teaching position by joining Mt. Sinai Primary Care Clinic as a clinical assistant in medicine and the emergency room. The appointment was obtained. The continued contact as an educational method is always timely in keeping pace. It was enjoyable in every sense and it materially advanced my pension finances. The teaching responsibilities were marginal—hands-on medical care, supervising medical students and residents. Whatever its motivation—travel, family needs, and the retirement from the medical responsibilities—initiated thinking on where and when the journey abides.

*   *   *

Sometimes the professional and personal overlap. Some of my preceding discussions in the journey speak for my detached or focused personality and/or attitude. That attitude can be voluntary or involuntary. As asserted previously, there certainly was intention for detachment. It aided in the down times and in the up times. I certainly found it wise and necessary during both my introduction to medicine and certainly during times when the observer was just as valuable as the practitioner (sometimes even more so). However, there were inseparable moments when the two functions merged—and one or the other dominated. One such episode occurred during the latter part of my years as a consulting physician and an observer.

Betty and I were to attend a formal affair. We elected to have dinner prior to attending the event and had reservations at a local restaurant consistent with the time for the celebration. It's good to highlight that we were in our attire of the moment. There was always the need for certain times when Betty and I could enjoy an evening away from the requirements of caring for our large family at dinnertime. It's always a distinct pleasure to have a date with your wife and share the affectations of time and place.

Dinner was served. At almost that precise moment, an episode of choking at a nearby six-member table ensued. Following a prolonged period of coughing, stability seemed likely. I journeyed to that table to inquire if all was well. An uncomfortable silence followed. I suggested a visit to a local Emergency Room as wise. I joined him on his way and all was well. His chest x-ray was normal and we returned to the restaurant.

Upon my return, the owner expressed gratefulness by inviting us to enjoy dinner at his expense. As I sat down with my wife, she shared some specific and pertinent information. Apparently, one of the party of six recently had been an observer to a fatal choking incident and there was general concern that this could recur. The sense of alarm was acute. Further, I had been recognized independently in that within the past month I had a professional consultation to a member of a family of one of the guests at the table on an entirely different medical matter. I was easily recognized in that black consulting physicians were rather rare in my time frame of local experience. It's easy to guess that I stand out for whatever reason.

Further, my timing and opportunity seemed to follow my star. The gentleman who precipitated the need for medical attention happened to be a relatively important banker. Within approximately two to three weeks I received a personal thank you from him and a note, "You have a friend at Chase Manhattan Bank." I never used the invitation but it does signal how timing and opportunity can fuse.

*　　*　　*

Suddenly in this the last quarter of the narrative, there is an awareness pending that the telling of the rest is more entwined and generated inward as well as outward. Sensations of the formative/middle/academic/ professional progress were filled with numerous emotional surges involved in traveling, family, and home. The maintenance of sequential development is in the narrative. There is an area of the present and past journey that should be explored.

The passage of time and effort during my internship, residency, and teaching years has a striking construct in my opinion. Betty, when joining the path to graduation and residency, filled the support system that emerged for the family and in personal areas to fulfill the journey.

Primarily, it's the presence of her educational background with a master's degree in developmental psychology from Columbia. Her employment opportunities were legion and rewarding on the financial front. Her income was able to allow us to enter the real estate market as owners. We purchased our first home in Garden City Park. Therefore, in spite of the meager earnings during the internship and resident years—the time-honored salary of $40 per month—we managed sparingly but adequately with raising a family of four children.

Of course, after the second year of training, covering for some local physicians on vacations was a fair supplement in the final year of my residency in internal medicine. In retrospect, the times were healthy for future dialogue. The memories were uniquely positive. Further, that first house in Garden City Park served as the site of the initial medical office for my practice. That evolved in 1962. It's memorable how the sense of timing continued to supervene when preparation and opportunity converge. That first adventure in housing and real estate satisfied all needs of the family until we moved to Jericho in 1969.

However, the significance of the first purchase and enlarging family cannot be overstated. The transfer to living in mid-Long Island provided a firm base with a 1.5 acre area and wide space for play. The house had been formerly owned by the Barrymore family. It was an old and colonial structure with sixteen rooms, several baths, and multiple garages and was located next to a high school of markedly high reputation. It was signal in that private school attendance could be avoided and therefore the family financial structure was protected for the future. Approximately 90% of Jericho high school student graduates successfully went on to college and/or graduate work. We considered ourselves fortunate. When we sold the home in the year 2000 we were well-rewarded.

For thirty+ years we stayed in residence and there were many positive events. "Jericho" became a noun with our friends and family—past and present. Certainly it served as a gathering place for our four sons and accumulated acquaintances during their coming college and graduate school experiences. Clearly we miss Jericho with all its pleasures. Currently, our sons have no place to gather for the times of celebration or holiday. Yes, we miss Jericho. Although bric-a-bracs from the house presently adorn the homes of all of our boys, those left in New York or in other areas are now distant.

*   *   *

It is timely to discuss some aspects of our four sons and their present lives.

The oldest son, Wayne, owns his own home near us in Florida and works at Florida Institute of Technology as a Master Mechanic. He formerly worked with the Department of Transportation in New York State. His assertion that he can fix any motor or machine is no idle boast.

Next in line, Mark, filled in a medical career. He is currently employed as an Emergency Room physician within the Long Island Jewish Division in Central Nassau County at Valley Stream Emergency Facility.

The third son, Drew, is a member of the New York bar and has extensive financial experience as a certified broker. Drew, in my opinion, demonstrated a degree of courage in 2005 when he ran for Mayor of Glen Cove on the Republican line. He was unsuccessful, but his endeavor was a source of pride and was very encouraging to me.

The fourth son, Ward, was born in the last year of my residence in training in 1962. He functions at an executive level as a certified financial advisor with the E-Trade commercial organization. Ward recently purchased a home in Atlanta, Georgia. He is a great source of pride to me and his mother.

During the time of the family growth, two avenues bore emphasis—education and travel. The latter became part of the family motif. The boys properly embraced our mantra for their education without undue stress on their parents. We, as parents, involved them in our thirst for travel. They accompanied us on two Caribbean cruises to South America and the Panama Canal. There was a memorable trip to Lima, Peru wherein the name "Fonrose" was stenciled on a restaurant wall on New Year's Day of 1971. The family also spent a month in a seaside villa in Portugal in 1971.

As a twosome, Betty and I visited several European cities with wonderful memories, such as:

Paris . . . We were walking down a Paris boulevard following a five-course dinner with wine, which was purely by accident. Betty does not drink but nevertheless, the dinner was a memorable event.

Rome . . . We were invited by a guide to dine with some Romans at a local bistro. Betty almost got pinched.

Venice . . . There was a decidedly dark midnight ride on the gondolas we'll never forget since the waterways were not lit—the midpoint was fearful.

London . . . This was truly memorable in that it involved passage on the QEII with return to JFK airport via a 3-3/4 hour ride on the Concorde.

This was followed by passage to Greece and a one-day stay in Piraeus.

There was an interesting meeting with an Italian couple who met in Rome and subsequently married. The fact that we were invited to their wedding in New York City and they visited us in Jericho is striking and singular. Travel has some exciting episodes interwoven with experience.

It can be borne out in this narrative that Betty, myself and the family have pursued travel with earnestness and vigor. During the times when the boys were in college (since our finances were exhausted with tuition) we would sit in Jericho and recall these adventures that we had recorded. We had to wait years until Drew graduated from law school before we could resume travel, our family pleasure.

As these recordings demonstrate, the travel and education were an appropriate part of our journey and they involved the entire family. There are other futures that will remain untold.

*   *   *

Just prior to the sale of Jericho, the period spent at Mt. Sinai on the Elmhurst campus was in transition. Some of our vacations were spent in Florida. The environment there seemed amenable to the reduced urgency of retirement. Melbourne seemed attractive. A small vascular ischemic episode tended to decide that my forty-five years of energetic function would have to suffice. The proactive health status has remained stable but the constriction of activity to a casual game of golf and daily walking seem both credible and wise. Clinical work at Mt. Sinai primary care clinic ended in 1998.

In retrospect, the decision was probably premature, since some of my health has remained quite stable. The residual of the illness is more in terms of mental and/or self-esteem rather than physical ability. The day to day activity prior to 1998 easily could be maintained.

There's more sustained work and function on this narrative than was ever done in the previous five to ten years before retirement. It took a long time before a truly bad decision was made during the journey from formative to the recent past. In retrospect, I don't recall ever making a backward decision. Every decision that I made for the 80 years starting in Trinidad always had a forward thrust and I regret retiring too soon. It was probably self-indulgent.

Notwithstanding, there is a sense of completion. The final phase planned is to employ some concepts on memory, recall, and streams of consciousness as they may apply finally to this 80 year passage of time.

If I may indulge in a bit of sentiment, there is much association with ideas or streams of conscious and non-conscious through the ruminations of Proust and *Swann's Way*. Nineteenth century thinking on inner directional thinking was prominent. Its prominence grew and had not receded until the onset of psycho-therapeutic pharmacology.

I'm mindful that this narration and its attempt at co-mingling emotion and memory may have an amateurish tone. In that light, I request scientific understanding.

PHOTOGRAPHS AND MEMORIES

THE FORMATIVE YEARS

✳   ✳   ✳

My mother Amoy, age 18, when she met my father, Gerald
1921

My mother and father on their wedding day
1925

My mother, my sister Baby doll (age 2) and me (age 4)
1929

My grandmother in Trinidad
She was approximately 58 years old when I arrived

Aunt Liz in Trinidad

Uncle Cornel
This photo was taken after my return to the United States

Baby Doll
(wearing a Shirley Temple outfit from my grandmother)
and me

As a young boy in Trinidad

Baby Doll in her teenage years

Tranquility Boys' Government Intermediate School Cricket Team
Winners of the Bonanza 2nd Class Cup
I am in the first row on the left (sitting cross-legged)
1940

My father and my grandfather at the beach in New York
This was taken while I was in Trinidad
1930-1940 timeframe

My grandfather in New York City
This is my grandfather who I went to visit when I was
admitted to medical school
1920-1930 time frame

My father in Rhode Island where he was working as a chauffeur
while my sister and I were in Trinidad
1935-1940 timeframe

Four Roads Trolley
The Four Roads Trolley line ended where I lived in Trinidad

THE MIDDLE YEARS

This photo was taken in Van Cortland Park in the Bronx where my father had taken me to play cricket just two weeks prior to my enlistment in the United States Navy as a pharmacist mate.

I am wearing a necktie around my waist instead of a belt as I did when I was a boy in Trinidad

1946

Baby doll, my father, and me
Long Island, New York
1946

THE ACADEMIC YEARS

A contemplative, earnest, pre-med student
This picture of me was taken on the front steps of the home
of my friend
Harold Heath during my time at Adelphi University
1949/1950

Graduation Day with my father
This marked the first of the Fonrose clan
to matriculate from a major university
Adelphi University
1952

Graduation Day with Dolie McQuinney Adams,
my long-time mentor and benefactor
Adelphi University
1952

Photo with Dolie McQuinney Adams on my wedding day
December 1956

My father, me, and my Uncle Lionel (my mother's brother)
Howard University College of Medicine
Graduation Day
June 5, 1958

Photo with Baby Doll
Howard University College of Medicine
Graduation Day
June 5, 1958

Photo with Beryl
Where inspiration and ambition merged
Howard University College of Medicine
Graduation Day
June 5, 1958

The woman in the front row on the right wearing the
wide-brimmed hat is Mary Cunningham, who I rented a room
from during my years at Adelphi University

Mary was the one who said to her holiday party guests,
"This is Harold, who is on his way to becoming a doctor."

Howard University College of Medicine
Graduation Day
June 5, 1958

Howard University College of Medicine
Class of 1958

I am in the fourth row—first one on the left
My good friend, Russell Minton, is in the 6th row—third from the
left

Aerial view of the quarters at the Los Angeles Port
of Embarkation during World War II which became
Harbor General Hospital in 1946
I referred to these Quonset huts upon my arrival
in California to start my residency

It was my first year of internship and I was working
every other night and every other weekend.
On the first weekend I had off, I took Betty to a Christmas Formal
given by a friend, Mervin Dymally, who went on
to become a Congressman and a U.S. Representative
intimately involved in African Affairs during his career and
subsequently became the Lieutenant Governor of California
under the administration of Governor Jerry Brown
in the mid-1980s.

1958

Internship Class Photo
Harbor General Hospital
July 1959

THE PROFESSIONAL YEARS

*   *   *

This is my favorite picture of Betty, reading to Wayne and Mark.
It's always how I envision her when she was with the children

**Birthday celebration with Betty, Aunt Marie and our boys,
Drew, Mark, Ward, and Wayne**

Wayne, Mark, Drew, and Ward

Aunt Marie with Drew and Wayne at Jones Beach in New York

One of my close friends, Russell Minton, sitting on the steps
of our front porch in Garden City Park, Long Island
This is our home where I had set up my practice in the lower level
1965-1968 time frame

Family photo at the Jericho home
Betty, me, Wayne, Ward, Drew and Mark

Aunt Marie
This picture represents several of the
Thanksgiving and Christmas holidays that she spent with us in
Jericho

Vacationing in Greece
1971

Mark's Graduation from Howard University
College of Medicine
1987

The four Howard University Medical School Graduates
Russell F. Minton, Jr.—Class of 1958
Russell F. Minton, Sr.—Class of 1929
Harold A. Fonrose—Class of 1958
Mark Fonrose—Class of 1987

Dancing with Aunt Marie
Late 1980s

My library at the Jericho home
I spent 80% of my time in this chair

Mark, Wayne, Drew, and Ward in the library
of our home in Jericho
1980s

Wayne, Ward, and Mark
1980s

Drew, Mark, Wayne, and Ward
1990s

Mark, Ward, and Drew
1990s

Alaska Trip
1990

Betty, myself, Wayne and Russell Minton
Christmas at the Jericho Home
1994

Betty and Russ Minton at our Jericho home

Drew's political campaign photo
2005

This was taken on a cruise ship on the Indian Ocean
travelling from Hong Kong to Australia
1991

This was taken at our Jericho Home

**Our 50th wedding anniversary
2006**

Oil painting of our home in Jericho

Summer photo of our home in Jericho

Winter photo of our home in Jericho

RECOGNITION AND APPRECIATION

T HE ISSUE OF ACKNOWLEDGEMENT IS approached cautiously, because my original thinking was that the completion of the journey would occur at the end of the narrative and there would be closure of the embedded memories. But the stirring continues. There is a need to identify personalities along the journey—all important—and in some specific manner in its adaption to the journey and they are so listed.

* * *

There is no direct intention to ignore the multiple persons who may recall my passage through any of the years discussed. I request their understanding of any omissions—it is truly regrettable. Embedded memory can be overlooked. For that, my apology is there for the asking.

* * *

My signal and special reference and major contribution to the journey narrative goes to my sister, *Lillian "Baby Doll" Porter*, who presently resides in Melbourne, Florida, within walking distance of my home. This is special since Baby Doll started with me on the move to Trinidad upon the passing of our mother in 1932. The reasons for the departure from the United Stated are fully referenced in the initial description of the early years. The history of our arrival in Trinidad is therefore part of her passage of the time spent in Four Roads. Her recall and impressions are different from mine. The differences arise out of the way male and female children were cultivated. Her experience and adaptations in the intervening years have a different tone and/or vigor than mine in the formative and foundation years.

The contribution of my sister to the journey can be measured in a specific sense. Other than Dolie McQuinney Adams and my wife, Betty, my sister Baby Doll is the single personality whose financial contribution can be referred to as decisive. The rent of approximately thirty dollars per month for the two-year stay in Cornell during graduate school was her special contribution. Graduate school and work on my master's degree at Cornell could not have been possible in her absence. In the light of her occupational background at that time, it probably equated to her whole month's salary. The reference of a major contribution is probably an understatement, and so there is true pleasure in this acknowledgment!

*　　*　　*

As acknowledgments are approached, the conceptuality of first and foremost comes to mind. **Ms. Shelley Johnson**, as mentioned earlier, provided me a distinct honor in spending her energy and time surveying the initial transcript prior to publication.

Her comments and criticisms were salutary and encouraging. Her insight on titling aided a major measure on my anxiety and appropriateness for which there is a manifest respect. In particular, there was her aid in assembling some of the philosophical challenges embedded in the title. My own comments on the title are an attempt to embody her reservations, but her criticisms also help that my point on memory remained in focus. Memory was always the ultimate intention. There is hope that there is no philosophical conflict in "the journey".

Also, at my request, Shelley accepted the challenge of writing an introduction as expressed in the Foreword.

*　　*　　*

Acknowledgments would be incomplete without mentioning Betty's Aunt Marie. **Marie Williams** represents the surrogate mother to Betty as my grandmother did with me. Aunt Marie also came to visit when we were in California and made the return trip with Betty and myself when we traveled from west to east for the return to my New York residency. Marie was accompanied by her husband, Bob Williams, on that trip.

Marie became a solid part of our six-member family from that point until her death in 2004 at the age of 104. Betty was fortunate enough to be able to prepare the celebration of her 100th birthday in Springfield, Ohio where the family journeyed to join in this celebration. Marie had served as a nurse in that area for approximately 50+ years. A host of friends and family recorded her rich life as a graduate registered nurse and religious leader.

Marie accepted the continued role of surrogate grandmother for my four sons as well as a mother-in-law for me. Over the years from 1962-2002, Marie supported our busy lives in New York and several cruises and summer vacations spent in Florida in the closing periods of my active medical career. She would travel back to Jericho with Betty and me, therefore in all of the ensuing years Marie spent Thanksgiving and Christmas with us. Several tales of her years were recited. During these conversations, my journey to that moment in time was recalled. Because of these descriptions of my times in Trinidad up to the present, it was Marie who first suggested and finally insisted that the journey of my life be recorded. She was one of many but in truth, she was the first enabler of this effort to describe the course of the journey and I acknowledge her confidence. It has certainly aided my need to continue this on to completion.

Again, it should be recognized that Aunt Marie spent many falls and winters with us in Florida, in the community where Betty and I have retired. Several of our present friends will probably appreciate her inclusion in the latter part of my journey of memories. The picture in this book of me dancing with her illustrates her happy way and the measure of joy she provided all who were in her presence. Memory *is* the true value!

*　*　*

Certain friends can be a witness. Starting in Trinidad, there are a few boyhood companions of special recall. During those early years, the open competition in all areas of training could be cited, whether it was sports, sportsmanship, academics, or schoolyard games. Some stood out, some others did not, but **Reginald Lewis** was part of the circle to which some attention is appropriate. His effect was integral and inspiring.

It is with some of this fondness that I visited Reginald when I last visited Trinidad in 2009 on a cruise. It was remarkable that he stated he followed my life throughout the years. His recall of the journey of the middle years went beyond and to the present. This was unnerving, but there was a compliment of interest that was compelling. Because of this our friendship can be marked as memories. The theme of the narration is felt to be validated. Why Reggie would choose to remember me is striking and endearing. The contribution to the idea of development of the formative years can be elevated, but they should not be discarded at will. The issue of whether these friends can serve as a marker for memory and progress can be discussed.

*　*　*

Other contacts can be mentioned from the middle years, specifically those I met during my time in the navy. Though critical, in retrospect they appear less personal and more formal.

* * *

The friendship of note that did develop in the middle years is the one I have referred to as one of conversational and Socratic activity. Her friendship was invaluable. ***Beryl***, a mother of two children, has already been described in my journey. Here the memories are very close to the surface and can be easily aroused since they were never embedded.

* * *

There is recall of the start of my work at Adelphi College in 1948 and leads to another long-term friendship critical at that juncture of the journey with a major impact at that moment. In retrospect, it was also a period of aloneness that was marked and vivid. ***George and Midge Rubin*** became, by accident of time and place, integral to the progress that followed. They fulfilled a pronounced intellectual and societal void in the period 1948-1952. There was active intercourse in the social structure of the time. George was preparing for podiatry school and Midge became a photographer of immense skill. They were present at my marriage as I was at theirs. George and Midge, in my view, represented the foremost feature of communication in those years following WWII. I recognize a penchant for long-term friendships. Theirs stands out as an example of how an accidental friendship may have an enduring positive impact. Chance and time merge in the classic sense for my benefit. We are still close friends living full lives with distance being the only separation. I marvel at my ever-present luck. The intellectual discussions of that period continue to be a fruit because of George and Midge Rubin. The past merges through the present, which is now our future.

This is an instance where memories push forward as acknowledgment proceeds. That period of vigorous interchange of ideas was most enlightening. Concepts of balance and judgment became part of the personality that later provided the base of responsible leadership with special reference to the practice of medicine. There is a sense of distinct honor to have known Midge and George over the past 60 years. Their friendship is viewed as an essential part of the journey and determinative in its total structure of the middle years to the past, the present, and the future of now.

* * *

Further, an enduring friendship made during the middle years can be defined as the timely meeting with **Fenton and Dottie Sands** and their family. As mentioned previously, we met in the early morning of my arrival at Ithaca seeking housing at the beginning of my two-year stay at Cornell and graduate school.

It is important to mention that Fenton was an original member of the Tuskegee Airmen Group established during World War II. He eventually wound up in the World Bank with Bob McNamara, the first defense secretary under President Kennedy. His interest in aviation possibly led to his involvement in the initial planning for the Orlando, Florida airport upon his retirement in the Florida community. When I began to visit Florida in the 1990s, I realized Fenton and his family had retired here and in the year 2000, my family retired in Florida as well.

When we met again, after the passage of nearly forty years, there was a sense of, "Well done." Our dreams and aspirations were well-realized and we therefore thoroughly enjoyed each other because of the measure of success derived through our hard work. Fenton was eventually recognized as an outstanding Cornell graduate by the Cornell Board of Trustees in the mid-1990s. Betty and I were thrilled to be in attendance on this occasion of his commendation.

Recently we were privileged to entertain his widow, Dorothy, at our home in Melbourne, Florida. Dorothy now resides in a retirement community in Macon, Georgia. Previously we had attended her 90th birthday celebration with her huge family. We still remain in close contact up to the present and I'm sure there will be other moments to share in the future.

*　　*　　*

In the category of friends of the journey, last but probably foremost, is the 50+ years of an enduring friendship with **Russell Minton**, my classmate at Howard University Medical School and constant companion in the years that followed. Russ and I started as roommates in 1954 at Carvell Hall. The dialogue in all areas has been vigorous, always informative, always factually developed, and always firm in conviction. Our time and discourse has been spent in outright argument, but with respect. All measures of persons should have such force to balance their opinions during presentation to the world, be they medical as in this instance, or for the general culture.

It is not possible for me to think of any event in the course of the past fifty years where Russell could not give a factual analysis of the events of the past with us. Our respect for each other has, in my opinion, been that integrated. The factors of this friendship remain well-known in our families. It is not possible to complete this geological sketch without discussing this friendship. Every single memory of those years is mixed with some measure of recall—directly or indirectly—relating to an event at which Russ is an integral part. To remember is to recall Russell!

Memory and recall are irrevocably entwined with Russell, Betty, and the entire Minton family. There is a natural flow to our friendship. Our families have always been part of the whole exposure, including one occasion in particular at Christmas time, when we celebrated four generations of physicians who had graduated from Howard Medical School from 1931-1987. Our friendship is wholesome and enduring to the present day.

*　　*　　*

As memories are again stirred from a desire, it is with this desire I recognize major accomplishments in my career and its enhancement with special reference to the time period in 1960 when the evolution of geriatric care was just a vague vision for the aged population.

That vision was probably well encapsulated in a governmental activity in the creation of the ***A. Holly Patterson Home for the Aged and Infirm*** in Uniondale, New York. The county executive was certainly far ahead of the medical thinking of that time and through the Department of Social Services and the Long Island community, found a better way to care for the indigent and infirm. Until that time, nursing home care was entirely domiciliary. The county executive's imagination was for an improved quality of both nursing and medical supervision. Thus was the eventual creation of a magnificent structure for the institutional care of the aged of approximately 900 residents (specifically *residents*, not *patients*) in 1960-1961. The structure was large and imposing. It was similar to the adjacent Meadowbrook County Hospital (where my full nighttime work occurred from 1948-1952) and in context of the day. There were four floors and on each floor was an open ward and private rooms. The private rooms were a major advancement in terms of the challenges for nursing home residents. The structure and intent was clearly ahead of contemporary thinking. The concept was therefore implemented and timely and a challenge for nursing, medical, and administrative adaptation.

The nursing derivative and responsibility fell to the first director of nursing, a lady by the name of *Ann Bowker*. By her own testimony, the empty building needed all the items from bedpans to sheets. There were hotel features of laundry, dietary needs, and housekeeping. Staffing of the nurses was part of the initial assignment. Finally, the compliment of approximately 750 nursing personnel fulfilled a major requirement.

Obviously, there was an equal need for administration of this burgeoning geriatric need. My sincere hope is that my citing of *Monroe Mitchell* receives his approval. His success of this venture was demonstrated by the fact of his recognition as the young administrator of the year, which I believe was in 1970. The exact memory of these events sometimes fades. I request his indulgence.

The medical needs were arranged by the appointment of its first medical director, *Lyndon Davis, M.D*. It was via his recruitment that my journey in practicing medicine began as a part-time consultant for the care of the aged. The concept of geriatrics had not evolved in 1963. The fact of my evolution to medical director in 1971 proceeded naturally. However, the full personality of the culture and compassion of the principal of optimum care was well-fixed in the gestalt of the institution. The nursing staff well-understood their mission! Because of that recognition, my description of 1963-1970 was that the Director of Nursing had created an institution for which she could be everlastingly proud.

My tenure was to continue and improve. Certainly, I hope that could be part of my legacy. The fact that there was a principal in the education and teaching program directed to both physicians and nursing which led to my advancement to the Fellowship in the College of Physicians may speak positively to that period of activity in geriatric medicine.

Any recall of the significance of the function of medical supervision at the Geriatric Center would be incomplete without the acknowledgement of the activity of my secretary, *Ms. Rennie Bloom*, in the years 1971-1986. Ms. Bloom provided overall management of my office. There was her ability to collate several of the minutes, staff conferences, memos, and supervisory directions. Her ability to recall any specific of dialogue and articles for my quick reference was of immense importance. The role of the medical director in a skilled nursing facility was outlined in an article published in the *American Journal of Geriatrics* in 1971. The significance of that article could be measured by the several requests for reprints as the years of medical practice evolved.

To Ms. Bloom is offered my eternal gratitude for her energy and diligence which maintained a stable course in these years leading to my retirement in 1986. It is my sincere hope that she remains well and functioning as I have.

* * *

Any attempt at acknowledgment could cite the **multiple secretaries and nurses** who may recognize both the time and place of my passage through the frame of the middle years at Cornell University, Meadowbrook Hospital, Harbor General Hospital and my tour as a disability consultant and other areas described in my career.

* * *

A recent personality discovered during my visits and final permanent stay in Florida could be cited in the fellowship developed with **Belford Carter**. Bel has been a constant golfing protagonist. He refuses to give my handicap the appropriate value—for that I forgive him.

During highlights of that journey, his encouragement that my journey be recorded has been his constant advice and encouragement. This literary attempt at recording was not easily enjoined. There is constant surprise on my part that completion has become a reality.

* * *

The advancement of this project could not have been completed without the guidance and encouragement of **Ms. Karen Rinehimer**. The fact of how she came to my aid represents a clear instance of timing, chance, and opportunity. Her business listing was in the local phone directory. The call was answered. The project began slowly and progressed capably to conclusion. My memory was all about the early confusion regarding how to proceed. My every difficult and apparent construction was solved and soothed by Karen's overwhelming assertion, "That can be fixed." It was encouraging and progress continued. If the project enjoys any measure of success, it is due to her diligence and professional excellence. Always, my luck and timing has prevailed in the background of diligence and hard work.

* * *

Let me extend my personal thanks to the professional critic of the final text, which I requested Ms. Rinehimer to obtain for a review in terms of clarity and substance of my interpretation of Marcel Proust's essay, *Remembrance of Things Past*. That review was provided with diligence and sincerity of effort. My feeling is that there is improvement of the final product in both clarity and meaning. My amateurish style needed correction and flow, which I believe was received.

It is my sincere hope that the narrative is readable and the substance available to any unknown general reader in terms of clarity and purpose, especially on the impact of memory. Of course, they will be the final judge of this offering for both context and purpose.

* * *

I would also like to give special thanks to **Stephen Dalla Costa** for his photo of the Four Roads Trolley as displayed on the cover of my book. It brought back another vivid memory of my childhood in Trinidad and I appreciate him granting permission to use his work.

* * *

Not all friends are here and my commentary about them is both polite and discretionary. Friends in human events have a natural life of context, derivations, and assessments. Within those phenomena, there is a reference to the term of friends as part of memory. In my mind, the term itself brings forth memories. The discourse is present in the journey and can appropriately be phased in as the passage or useful markers of friends encountered or accumulated along the way. Therefore, the area of the formative and middle years lends itself to a narrative description. It is entirely possible to use the pursuit of memory to identify a person or persons who stand in that clear light where they helped fashion that time and its evolution.

EPILOGUE

THE FLOW OF EVENTS UNFOLDS as memory from the initial spark. The spark—in view of its proximity to the other memories, events, and adjoining sparks—thereby causes a surge.

Memory is hardly an isolated event. Usually it's part of a composition of emotions or ideas. As each layer is removed, other features of the recall may be revealed. Unlayering proceeds as a natural evolutionary phenomenon. As previously stated at the outset of the narrative, the volume, energy, and power of the revealed memory can become part of the surge. This construct possibly continues to an eventual end as the passage ensues.

Here there may be resonance with the concept of a stream of consciousness, which concludes the inherent levels of the memory procedure. The procedure moves slowly and inevitably to the moment of stillness. The rush of ideas or consciousness reminds me in recall of cascading thoughts, simulating waves, receding and following with more waves of varying degrees of power. Waves covering waves or rivulets, each with decreased energy or volume, is the imagery.

Another type of imagery that produces a similar effect of descending force eventually leading to quiet may also be acceptable. Events and memory are viewed here as interchangeable and as part of the surge of memory and events conforming to the exit of adjacent memory. The unfolding begins and continues with full force, strong and persistent, as connectability continues layer by layer.

Memory unfolds starting with any probe at any part of the cycle, convenient or inconvenient. The memories could be characterized as a stream of consciousness with a surge having its separate volume or power. The additional mixture of energy, volume and layering recalls the cascading of an avalanche. As the surge unfolds, the unexposed power of recall and activity assumes functionality nearly devoid of the consequences of the initial probe. The process assumes its own validity and proceeds to a natural conclusion as the journey subsides, emotion and memory expended. But the quiet is deceptive. Recall stirred sometimes stays as motion.

The initial power starts with a naked force as it unfolds. Layer by layer that force initially increases then declines in force and volume. The power tends to diminish and lessen its thrust until both power and volume are quiet or appear unmoving.

The total could then be the stream of consciousness or avalanche that may appear to merge or coalesce to the quiet phenomena. Memory is then hushed and for a time both the memory and the journey concludes and a natural course of events and memory coincide. Memory again becomes remote and embedded, waiting for the next probe. From a mere personal perspective, the motion probably continues because of the surges of the journey. And so the turbulence of my memory recedes into *Swann's Way*.

The past unfolds from its background of memory—submerged, silent and vague. Any sensation can be revealed as a continuum of ideas—fact to fact, idea to idea, sensation to sensation—all touching and communicating through memory and stimulus, moment to moment.

At this point in the front which is producing a decreasing force, the energy dissipates itself to become embedded or no longer seen, but not gone. Each part of the whole maintains integrity to varying degrees.

The path of the memory may be approached as a surge, therein creating spontaneous pressure for it to emerge. There is the possibility of natural selection not unlike Darwin's Law.

The surge, however, may stimulate a conscious or subconscious stream of emotion. I submit that the stream of consciousness then simulates an avalanche of the embedded memory. The energy, starting with speed as a major force, with time and stimuli decreasing, loses some of its power. As it loses its power, it dampens out its volume and energy to near stagnation, but it may still be there—embedded—only to arise on an appropriate probe.

Avalanche of memory may subside but it lives on, waiting for a repeat impulse to discharge the memory.

So, there is no end, only memories.

FINAL THOUGHTS

E MBEDDED MEMORIES SEEM TO BE waiting . . . waiting. Silent but persuasive.

The stillness of the ebb tide is intriguing. Poised, silent and quiet following the cascading effect and tumult of the surge of memories and although calm, it suggests there may be more. And so, as the flow of events unfolds, it leaves bare memories of areas of the journey that could be commented on. Some early reviews of my initial writings suggest a conflict between the journey and my feelings along the way.

It strikes me that the surprise of a philosophical tone on my discussions of this eighty-year journey, wherein forty to fifty years of that time were on the way to a focused profession, would be productive for any structured personality. The quality of life of learning academics speaks for a philosophical approach which would persist in my personality as described. The idea of a long journey of life not being engaged as a philosophical exercise is indeed a conundrum. The opposite view where there is an inner person is sort of oblique. If "feelings" had become predominant in that period, the markings more likely might have escaped into psychiatry as a primary purpose to the dependent personality.

*　　*　　*

As the ebb tide unfolds, some fragments of memory emerge and the final stages conflict with prior memories. There seems to be silence following the tumult and crescendo and as that silence ensues—it waits for the next forceful stimulus. My request that Shelley Johnson, the daughter of Beryl, my inspirational college acquaintance with whom I shared dialogues of platonic and Socratic discourse, read my initial writings provided a renewal of some of these memories. Some concerns were of greater personal experiences vs. the intent of the narrative.

This stirred some of the internal concerns during the journey and the issue of my detached sheltered persona described to illuminate some of the need for focus and discipline in the middle years. The discussion of the recall of working ten to fourteen hours day/night could be cited. There was referral to that pattern emerging following the end of the naval career that led to preparation for college entrance, the four to six year period of undergraduate work, and the need to sustain that same pattern for the next ten years with full-time school attendance and full-time night work.

Some of my surprise in retrospect is that ten to fifteen continuous years was spent in full day time work and night time work. The end stage of extensive work in internship and residency followed. The net results were 15+ years of extensive activity.

*　　*　　*

I called this memoir *It's Only Money . . . Memory is the True Value* for good reason. In an attempt to explain the word *"memory"* in the titling of the book, the suggestion by Ms. Johnson was to place its analysis at the end of the narrative thereby providing a clarification of the word *"only"*.

Without memory, there is nothing. Zero. Zephyr. Memory serves the purpose of providing a background to the human condition and it's the ultimate insult to that condition when expressed in Alzheimer's disease as a terminal aspect of life. Shakespeare illustrated the idea forcefully in the essay, *All the World's a Stage*. The final remarks to the seven stages were, "Sans teeth, sans eyes, sans taste, sans everything."

There is the theoretical process that joins the role of memory as an *"only."* It rests as nothing since it is without any intrinsic energy, life, or force that is not intrinsic to "it". "It" (or money) could lie unattended, inert, and if unstimulated by something external, remain there. Thus, the concept of the word *"memory"* in the title, without which there is no specific purpose and self, remains embedded and unlived. Its existence is entirely dependent on the role assumed by the owner or possessor as a true commodity. The existence being its only task, thus the mantra, *"It's Only Money . . . Memory is the True Value."*

*　　*　　*

There is this view that there is a defining value about money. But in my mind, this view is vacant. It reflects an overwhelming product which is not exclusive. The statement that it makes is defining by its mere existence but there is a possible correlation and connectability between the exclusion of the word *only* in a haunting echo rendered in the Peggy Lee rendition of "Is that all there is?" That hollowness of intent is about money. This is an extreme position but still direct with regard to *It's only Money . . . Memory is the True Value* and reminds me of the question raised by the singer as an indistinct quantity, with money judged to be an inanimate object without real value but is assigned a significance that is only in the mind of the owner of the object. It is very likely to be false and pretentious without any merit or integrity of its own being assigned to the value and does not create any value of its own.

*   *   *

Because of the focus on memories, certain aspects of the original intent of the "telling" emerged in the challenges, both philosophical and practical, which started in other conversations. My wife, Betty, offered a practical explanation. "You and the journey are not separable!" The assertion that *it* is not *me* is not easily reconciled. On reflection, her remark is pointed and on the mark. In defense, I recall the daytime educational processes and full-time night work spanning that period of fourteen to fifteen years being a time of sustained stress. The last four years were spent in full-time training and every other day and every other weekend were on-call periods. This continued until the completion of residency training in 1962. That sense of responsibility only changed its focus; but the process for discipline was the same. That recognition is germane to the adaptation of detachment and an effort to maintain that personality of the journey for a long and sustained duration of 80+ years. Detachment and embodied persona became the stabilizing pattern. That pattern of the personality merged to become a relatively successful self. That personal adaptation developed over time so that the *me* could both function and survive! That it could now be embedded should be no mystery. My view is that it was a direct necessity. Compartmentalization became the enduring pattern.

*   *   *

Allowing memory to wander brings to mind the seamless manner with which each area of the narrative flows to the period preceding and following it. My recall is that the periods were seamless, natural, and without interruption. No episode stood alone or isolated, needing extensive and detached reference. Each blended with the other; the effect was part of the journey as a whole. In retrospect, there is resonance to the effect of memory and memories as described in the prologue. Each phase or phrase emerged independently, pushing itself to be part of the whole, while maintaining its own identity. The connectability of the preceding and the following energy, joined the active and philosophical integrity. And so, the formative, middle, and academic years form the purpose and integrity of the journey as a philosophical exercise or experiment.

* * *

In my opinion, the detached private personal integrity was needed for survival. There was little time for intense reflection in that there was a need for sustained focus to be maintained. Discipline was a foremost quality and was essential. In my estimation, as aforementioned, the foundation of the formative years was mandatory to a successful outcome. Focus and a detached personality worked and are construed as essential. Presently, the look back forced a sense of purpose and dedication. It is possible that a casual observer may feel there is too much philosophical tonality but this external observation I submit is the description of 80+ years being actively involved in a climb to professional achievement. *It* would indeed involve philosophical principles let alone the observation that recall of those years is a philosophical exercise in the purest sense. By definition, it is *thought* rather than *feelings* that suspend the activity of the memory to describe along the roadway. That passage seems presently to miss the significance of the journey. My admonition to my literary aide has been from the beginning, "This narrative is about *it*, meaning *the journey*. It's not about *me*." It is helpful that the mission is being accomplished. It's the *journey*, not the *person*.

* * *

It is not possible to overemphasize the structure of the journey during its discussion. Though by definition the journey is long, there is evidence for continuity beginning with the arrival in Trinidad. There is no practical separation of the formative years, the middle years, and academic years, and following years that led to the finality in retirement.

Each episode flows naturally from one to the other. There is no gap. There is total connectivity from each phase or phrase that is enjoined in life's journey. This is effectively demonstrated in the concept of memories and how they evolve. Yesterday's memory belongs to today and tomorrow. The journey is a continuous flow of events. Therefore the initiating phase—the flow of events—signals the onset. Each phrase may have greater significance in retrospect, but during the time when it's evolving, it is not possible to recognize one detail as being more important than the other if viewed in a background as a whole spectrum of events.

As the discussion on memory unfolds, that concept is again displayed where each memory—which may start as a separate focus—abuts, pushes, shoves, and displaces another one that comes along. Each tries to survive and maintain its identity. I feel that the basis of the dialogue—theoretically for the discussion of this journey—has been pronounced in *Remembrance of Things Past* and that's why I use that as the fulcrum of the ideological role that holds this journey together.

The summation of this idea and the philosophical concerns later in life are what bring back the memories.

This is my story . . . this is my song

Finally, the story evolves as a historical perspective of a young male arriving in a humble environment of Caribbean culture. There, ambitions and musings began. There, he was exposed to characteristics of determination, discipline and sustained diligence.

These features became embedded. These attributes forged his ambition to enter a structured profession to which at a later time he was able to provide an aspect of leadership in geriatric thinking. He has become convinced these features allowed his vision and aura of light on a distant horizon to come into sharp focus close-up. And the goal became available.

My firm conviction is that these similar, average characteristics are available to each and every subset of persons and culture. With particular and special reference to the future, I render a "shout-out" of encouragement.

BIBLIOGRAPHY AND REFERENCES

Cervantes, Miguel de, *The Ingenious Gentleman Don Quixote of La Mancha*, two volumes, 1605 and 1615;

Darwin, Charles Robert, (12 February 1809-19 April 1882). He established that all <u>species</u> of life have descended over time from <u>common ancestry</u>, and proposed the <u>scientific theory</u> that this <u>branching pattern</u> of <u>evolution</u> resulted from a process that he called <u>natural selection</u>.

Proust, Valentin Louis Georges Eugène Marcel *À_la_recherche_du_temps perdu* (*In Search of Lost Time*; earlier translated as *Remembrance of Things Past*), published in seven parts between 1913 and 1927.

Rousseau, Jean-Jacques (28 June 1712-2 July 1778). He was a <u>Genevan</u> philosopher, writer, and composer of 18th-century <u>Romanticism</u>. His <u>political philosophy</u> influenced the <u>French Revolution</u> as well as the overall development of modern political, sociological and educational thought.

Shakespeare, William, *As You Like It*, "All the world's a stage" is the phrase that begins a <u>monologue</u> from <u>William Shakespeare's *As You Like It*</u>, spoken by the melancholy Jaques in Act II Scene VII. The speech compares the world to a stage and life to a play, and catalogues the seven stages of a man's life, sometimes referred to as the seven ages of man: infant, schoolboy, lover, soldier, justice, <u>pantaloon</u>, and second childhood, "sans teeth, sans eyes, sans taste, sans everything".

Tolstoy, Leo, *War and Peace*, 1869. Russkii Vestnik

Discography

LEIBER, JERRY and STOLLER, MIKE, "Is That All There Is?", written in the 1960s. Became a hit for American singer Peggy Lee from her recording in November 1969.

CPSIA information can be obtained at www.ICGtesting.com
Printed in the USA
BVOW08s1222170515

400693BV00001B/96/P